WILTON WOMEN

GW00645295

Wilton Women

Chatelaines, Saints and Pioneers

Best wishes,

Russ Foster

Mian Fost

R E AND M S G FOSTER

THE HOBNOB PRESS

First published in the United Kingdom
by The Hobnob Press,
8 Lock Warehouse, Severn Road, Gloucester GL1 2GA
www.hobnobpress.co.uk

British Library Cataloguing in Publication Data
A catalogue record for this book is available from the British Library

ISBN 978-1-914407-36-9

Typeset in Adobe Garamond Pro 11/14 pt
Typesetting and origination by John Chandler

Front cover: detail from Philip, 4th Earl of Pembroke, and his family by Sir Anthony van Dyck, c. 1635
Back cover: Lady Pembroke and evacuees, 1940

Contents

List of Illustrations

Unless stated otherwise, all images appear courtesy of Lord Pembroke and the Wilton House Trustees.

Preface and Acknowledgements

B OOKS ABOUT WILTON HOUSE, who lives there, and
what lies within it, are like buses. Beginning in 1906, Lord
Stanmore published a two volume life of Sidney, Lord Herbert of
Lea. Readers then had to wait more than thirty years before another
Lord Herbert, the future 16th Earl of Pembroke, published two
volumes of letters and diaries (1939 and 1950) relating to the life
of his ancestor, the 10th Earl. Nearly another generation would
elapse before Sir Tresham Lever wrote *The Herberts of Wilton*,
(1967) the first full history of the family. Hot on its heels, in 1968,
the 16th Earl published a catalogue of the family's paintings and
drawings. However, a further hiatus, this time approaching half a
century, went by until a comparative avalanche of titles appeared.
R.E. Foster's *Sidney Herbert*, the first full length biography of any
male member of the family, appeared in 2019. Early in 2020 it
was followed by Peter Stewart's definitive catalogue of the art
and sculpture collection, the first part of a 'Wilton Trilogy'.[1] The
others, published the same year, were Francis Russell's updated
catalogue of the paintings' collection, and John Martin Robinson's
overview of the history of the house.

Why, therefore, a fifth volume in four years? Firstly, the
present study is intended very much for the general reader,
certainly for a wider audience than might be attracted by more
academic tomes. Secondly, it is not, as all but one of the above
volumes is, written by a member of the Herbert family or, by
somebody who has, to some degree, been commissioned by them.
Above all, the book is offered as a first essay in filling what so
obviously appears to us as a lacuna: the part played by women
in Wilton's story. Sir Tresham Lever's book is the most culpable

1   J.M. Robinson, *Wilton House*, p. 258.

in this respect. Catherine Woronzow, for example, who became the second wife of the 11th Earl in 1808, merits only a single mention in its index, yet she was integral to a major re-fashioning of Wilton House and the mother of the son from whom the current line of the Herbert family descends. Such omissions are the more inexcusable given that Wilton, far more so than is the case for most boroughs, has seen women playing prominent, even dominant, parts in its history. For the purposes of this book, therefore, the gentlemen have been respectfully requested to surrender their seats to the ladies.

Our original idea was to limit our study to the Countesses of Pembroke. It very soon became apparent, however, that this was insufficient: some Countesses made little impression at Wilton; conversely, several women who never became Countess, made a considerable impact. Whilst, therefore, the Countesses remain the main focus of our attention, we have allowed ourselves a certain degree of latitude. Some will object that we have been too idiosyncratic in our selection. Others will say that we have been guilty of countless breaches of etiquette in the way we engage with them. For this we claim the reader's indulgence: it was always our intention to be more latter-day John Aubrey than the most recent edition of *Debrett's*.

William, 18th Earl of Pembroke, current holder of the family title, has in no way sought to influence what we have written, but we would very much like to thank him, and Lady Pembroke, for the enthusiasm with which they greeted our project. We are especially grateful to them, and the Wilton House Trustees, for allowing us to use images in their care. In sourcing material for the text, we are indebted to the staffs of the National Archives at Kew, the British Library, the Bodleian Library in Oxford, Wiltshire and Swindon History Centre in Chippenham, West Sussex Record Office in Chichester, the University of Southampton, and Salisbury Library.

Those working behind the scenes at Wilton whose assistance and insights, both formal and informal, have furthered our endeavours include Chris Rolfe, Nigel Bailey and Craig Webster.

Spurred on by the prospect of impending retirement, Charlotte Spender, in particular, went above and beyond the call of duty in tracking down a veritable host of family photographs and paintings. Our friends and colleagues on the guiding team have contributed much through lively debate and disagreement about Wilton's women over several years; and doubtless much more by a process of osmosis.

Our daughter, Susanna, employed sharp eyes in eradicating numerous errors from the text. No less helpful has been the forensic scrutiny subsequently afforded it by Susan Glynn. Last, and by no means least, we wish to acknowledge the help, advice and encouragement bestowed by John Chandler as the book went from conception to birth through his Hobnob Press.

A joint literary endeavour, especially one between husband and wife, might be thought inadvisable. We do not recommend it as a regular venture. It helps, at least, that we are both guides at Wilton House. So far as the division of labours is concerned, the initial idea and the title for the project that necessitated them, was Michaela Foster's. Broadly speaking, she has also taken the lead in writing part one; her lesser half, Ruscombe, in part two. The latter has also taken chief responsibility for the supporting apparatus of notes, bibliography and index. It is customary at the end of such paragraphs to say that the author assumes sole responsibility for any errors. Perhaps sufficient clues have been provided that the reader can apportion blame as she or he thinks appropriate?

Goathurst / Wilton, 11 April 2022

Prologue
The 'Herstory' of Wilton

WHAT IS WILTON? Over time it has been, variously, capital of a kingdom, landed estate, abbey, civic borough, parliamentary seat, county town, stately home, carpet manufactory and film location. It was settled by the Anglo-Saxons at least as early as the eighth century. By the ninth century it had become an important royal centre at the heart of the ancient kingdom of Wessex. Winchester supplanted it after 900 but Wilton remained as the administrative centre of the smaller unit known as Wiltshire. Relative decline thereafter became more pronounced as traffic and trade found easier passage at New Sarum (modern Salisbury), the foundation stone of whose cathedral was laid in 1220. Yet it was only from 1832 that Wilton ceased to be the county town.

For approaching five centuries now, however, Wilton has been chiefly famous for the stately home which dominates it, the Herbert family who inhabit it, and the Pembroke title which they assumed in 1551.[1] To date, in an unbroken line of succession, there have been eighteen Earls. Only one, William, 6th Earl, never married. Allowing for a few instances where there exists some ambiguity over whether a marriage had actually taken place according to English law, 26 women have married an Earl of Pembroke, though only 21 became Countess. Death, and less drastic forms of separation, explains the disparity. Of the Countesses, five were to enjoy the styling for ten years or fewer: Anne Parr, first wife of the 1st Earl, for only a few months, was

---

1 See Appendix 1.

easily the shortest lived in the title; next in that line, at six years, is
Katherine Talbot, second wife of the 2nd Earl.[1] By contrast, three
Countesses stand out for their remarkable longevity: Beatrice
Paget, wife of the 15th Earl, Countess for 47 years; Elizabeth
Spencer, wife of the 10th Earl, chatelaine at Wilton for 38 years,
and Octavia Spinelli, wife of the 12th Earl, who was Countess at
Wilton for 30 years, yet never set foot in the place!

Despite the fact that only three other Countesses enjoyed the
title for more than twenty years, they have generally been blessed
with strong constitutions. Elizabeth Beauclerk, first wife of the
11th Earl, and Anne Parr, the 1st Countess, were the unfortunate
exceptions: they were only 27 and 36 respectively when they
died, the former from complications following childbirth. One
might have expected the dangers of childbearing to have claimed
more victims. But no other Countess died under the age of 40.
Unfortunately, their husbands have not always been so blessed
with longevity: a number of Countesses have had to bear the
dignity of Dowager (the Dowager Countess traditionally went to
live at Bulbridge House, just outside the gates of Wilton Park) for
a considerable period of time. Seven did so for more than twenty
years. Henriette de Kérouaille, wife of the 7th Earl, was Dowager
for fully 45 years; Elizabeth Spencer, married to the 10th Earl, was
free of her husband for 37 years. Given what they both had had
to endure at the hands of their respective spouses, these lengthy
periods might strike the impartial reader as instances of poetic
justice.

The age at which Herbert wives married was germane less
to their prospects of becoming Countess than their likelihood of
producing the all-important 'heirs and spares'. The only two for
whom childbearing was not a consideration were Anne Clifford,
second wife of the 4th Earl, and Barbara Slingsby, second wife of
the 8th Earl: both were 40 and entering second marriages. They
were the exceptions that prove the rule that Herbert wives were

---

1   Katherine Talbot, second wife of the 2nd Earl, was probably in her
mid-twenties, but the year of her birth is uncertain.

usually young. The youngest, the match celebrated in van Dyck's great family portrait in the Double Cube Room, was that of Lady Mary Villiers, daughter of the Duke of Buckingham, to Charles, Lord Herbert, eldest son of the 4th Earl. The union had been agreed by their respective families in August 1626 when Lady Mary was four. By the time the marriage proper took place in January 1635 she was still only twelve; her husband positively ageing at fifteen. But since Lord Charles, who would have become the 5th Earl, succumbed to smallpox only a year later, Lady Mary never did become Countess. Of those who did, Mary Sidney was just sixteen when she became the third wife of the 2nd Earl in 1577; Lady Susan de Vere was seventeen when she became the first wife of the 4th Earl in 1604.

Most of the women under consideration were in their early twenties when they married. Although six never gave birth to children, or at least to any that survived beyond infancy, the others were a fecund body. Between them they were mothers to at least 73 children (35 sons, 38 daughters). That said, the numbers would be much smaller without the breeding machine that was Margaret Sawyer, first wife of the 8th Earl. She gave birth to twelve children between 1684 and 1706, most of whom survived into adulthood.

Raw data, however, whilst helping to provide context, is hardly the staple fare needed to enjoy the long journey travelled by the women who have contributed so much to the story of Wilton. It is their human stories that inform, illuminate, sometimes appal, and (hopefully) entertain. The way and the depth in which we can approach them is, inevitably, governed by the historical record: we cannot even be sure of the year during which some of our earliest subjects were born; by the time we reach the eighteenth century, by contrast, we can delve deeper and say with certainty what they ate and wore on a particular day.

Two of the women considered, Mary Sidney and Florence Nightingale, enjoy a global reputation. Four others, Anne Clifford, Elizabeth Spencer, Elizabeth à Court and Edith Olivier, have been deemed worthy of an entry in the *Oxford Dictionary of National Biography*. This is a fairly remarkable roll call. Certainly it is comparable, arguably more impressive, than the collective achievements of the Earls. None of the latter enjoys anything approaching a global reputation. It is true that ten of them have an entry in the *Oxford Dictionary of National Biography*, but this partly reflects the male and aristocratic bias of those who conceived that project in the late Victorian period. Some of their female counterparts, for instance Mary Fitzwilliam and Catherine Woronzow, were more worthy and deserve to be better known. Beatrice Paget, a larger than life character comparable to any of her predecessors as Countess, does not even have (the admittedly dubious honour) of an entry on Wikipedia. And of those that are better known, Elizabeth à Court in particular, should be afforded greater recognition than she currently receives.

There is an earlier history of Wilton, however, that makes both the womenfolk and the Herberts look like the arrivistes that they were. As is apt now to be forgotten, the ancestral family home of nearly five centuries was home to a community of nuns for over seven centuries: the twenty first century house sits, in large part, on the footprint of the abbey begun nearly a thousand years earlier. It would be obtuse in the extreme to embark on our main task without taking a short glance at that older 'herstory'. And so we shall begin, as we shall end, with the story of Edith.

Saint Wulfthryth and Saint Edith

WE CANNOT SAY for certain when an abbey first appeared in Dark Age Wilton: our primary source, a poem, dates only to the fifteenth century.[1] However, a chantry chapel founded c. 773, is credited to Wulfstan, a Wiltshire nobleman who was killed in battle in 802. Wulfstan's widow, Alburga, a half-sister of King Egbert of Wessex, persuaded Egbert to turn her husband's chapel into a convent for 13 nuns.[2] The Abbey was re-founded, and expanded to accommodate 26 nuns, by Alfred the Great of Wessex. This act of piety may well have been prompted by his having survived a sobering encounter with a large Viking army on a hill overlooking Wilton in 871.[3] During the tenth century, if not earlier, the Abbey gained a reputation as a centre of educational excellence, a sort of boarding school for upper class girls. Wilton was home not just to nuns but 'a safe repository for daughters whose status as assets or liabilities remained to be determined'.[4] Alumni would include two of King Alfred's granddaughters, Gunhild, daughter of King Harold II (killed at Hastings in 1066), and Maud, who married Henry I. It is two other women, however, who stand pre-eminent in the Abbey's history.

Wulfthryth, who could boast royal blood, was born c. 937. She was one of the many who entered Wilton, not as a nun, but as a member of its lay community. In 960, however, her schooling was interrupted by Edgar, King of the English. According to Goscelin of Canterbury, an eleventh century Benedictine monk and chronicler, 'The king loved her as Jacob loved Rachel;

1 R.B. Pugh & E. Crittall, (eds), *The Victoria History of Wiltshire*, III, pp. 231-42.
2 D. Farmer (ed), *The Oxford Dictionary of Saints,* p.11.
3 R. Abels, *Alfred the Great*, pp. 137-8.
4 S. Hollis (ed), *Writing the Wilton Women*, p. 327.

he had taken her, the splendid star of royal maidens, from the very schoolroom by divine dispensation, and united her with the kingdom by indissoluble vows'.[1] Goscelin evidently saw little amiss in Edgar's love-struck initiative; the king, after all, enjoyed the epithet of 'peaceable'. But he also earned a reputation as something of a sexual predator: Wulfthryth's sister had only recently escaped his attentions by taking sanctuary at Wilton. Then again, given the sisters' royal blood, Edgar's motives may have been, at least in part, dynastic. At any event, Wulfthryth found herself whisked off to Kent where she may or may not, willingly or otherwise, have married Edgar. What is not in dispute is that she gave birth to a daughter – Edith.

Wulfthryth, her marital status unclear, was allowed to return to Wilton two years later. Whether out of remorse or as reward, Edgar showered her with riches. Wulfthryth rose to become Abbess. She used the King's largesse to build a wall around the Abbey, to acquire relics, and to provide charity for the wider community.[2] Wulfthryth remained Abbess until her death in 1010. She was buried in front of the high altar; Goscelin described her as the 'hidden treasure and light' of the Abbey.

Wulfthryth would later be canonised but it was Edith, her daughter by King Edgar, who would become Wilton's patron saint. Taken by her mother to live with her in the Abbey, Edith was tutored by Radbod of Reims and Benno of Trèves, two eminent continental scholars engaged by the King. Goscelin depicted her as something of a polymath. Edith, he enthused, was endowed with an angelic voice, 'sweet eloquence, a capable intellect notable in all kinds of thought, a perceptive ardour in reading; hands as elegant as they were accomplished in painting and writing as scribe and author'.[3] She also developed a decidedly un-nun like penchant for fine clothes: the chronicler William of Malmesbury described them as having been luxurious and golden. When taken to task over the matter by Aethelwold, the Bishop of Winchester, however,

1   Hollis, *Writing the Wilton Women*, pp. 318-19.
2   *Oxford Dictionary of National Biography* (*ODNB*), 'St Edith'.
3   Hollis, *Writing the Wilton Women*, p. 311.

Edith was defiant: 'pride', she told him, 'may exist under the garb of wretchedness; and a mind may be as pure under these vestments as under your tattered furs'.[1]

Edith proceeded to demonstrate the truth of her contention. She 'was conspicuous for her personal service of the poor and her familiarity with wild animals'. Report suggests that she kept an animal sanctuary of sorts.

1. Saint Edith, probably 14th century (Wikimedia Commons)

Edith also resisted attempts to get her to abandon the relatively simple life at Wilton in order to make the most of her royal ancestry. Most notably, she subverted moves to have her appointed as abbess of the wealthy houses of Winchester, Barking, and Amesbury by nominating deputies to act in her stead. In 978, she even rebuffed overtures from some nobles of the realm to make her queen in her own right in succession to her murdered half-brother, King Edward the Martyr.[2]

Towards the end of her life, Edith provided physical proof of her piety by overseeing the construction – the design was part hers – of an oratory in Wilton (long since vanished) dedicated to St Denys. But she died, aged 23, on September 16th 987, only 43 days after it had been consecrated. Dunstan, the Archbishop of Canterbury, who had officiated, had unhelpfully prophesised her imminent demise.

A cult quickly developed around Edith's memory. Within a week of her death she was said to have appeared before her mother in a vision with the news that she had broken the head of the Devil. She appeared before St Dunstan more than a decade later to tell him that her body had not decomposed. Dunstan, in

1   Hollis, *Writing the Wilton Women*, pp. 47, 246. Edith, it should be emphasised, was a member of the secular community at Wilton. It is not clear that she intended becoming a nun.
2   Hollis, *Writing the Wilton Women*, p. 305.

tandem with Wulfthryth, decided to put the matter to the proof: 'fragrant perfumes gave off the breath of paradise' when her grave was opened. On the fast track to sainthood, Edith was canonised in 997. Wulfthryth, by then Abbess of Wilton, had her remains reinterred in the Abbey, which was rededicated in Edith's name.[1]

The Abbess apart, the Wilton community was initially ambivalent about its new saint. As has been pointed out, the historical Edith had done little for the Abbey. Wulfthryth, for one, did more. It was she who was buried in front of the altar in 810; Edith had been buried near the south porch. The key moment in transforming Edith's standing came when King Canute decided to venerate her memory in the 1040s: Edith had earned his gratitude (he prayed to her) by saving him from shipwreck during a storm as he crossed the North Sea. He repaid the gratitude by visiting Wilton 'with solemn gifts, and published this great miracle with prolific testimony'. The most tangible example of that testimony was a golden shrine.[2]

Edith's reputation, given her links to the Anglo-Saxon throne, could easily have diminished as a result of the Norman Conquest in 1066. But William the Conqueror himself soon became a benefactor of the Abbey. The nuns then consolidated their hold on Edith by commissioning Goscelin of Canterbury (c. 1080) to write her life. The result, *Vita Edithe*, was less biography than hagiography. His Edith is 'a reclusive mystic seeking union with her spiritual bridegroom', a far cry from the classy dresser who loved animals.[3] Amongst those impressed, however, was Edward I: he rebuilt and embellished Edith's shrine at the turn of the thirteenth century. As many as twenty churches may have been dedicated to her in the later medieval period.

---

1   Hollis, *Writing the Wilton Women*, p. 40.
2   Hollis, *Writing the Wilton Women*, pp. 270-1.
3   Hollis, *Writing the Wilton Women*, p. 276.

Isabel Jordayne and Celia Bodenham

THE STORY OF EDITH would have been impressed upon Gytha, daughter of Godwin, Earl of Wessex. She was, after all, brought up and educated in the Abbey. But she left it (and changed her name to Edith) when she married King Edward the Confessor, the last Anglo-Saxon king, in 1045. Proof of her piety, gratitude and wealth was demonstrated by her financing the rebuilding of the existing wooden abbey in stone. It was consecrated in 1065. The Abbey estate's income, as recorded in Domesday Book in 1086 was £245 15s. This made it the wealthiest nunnery in England.

After two centuries and more on a more or less uninterrupted spiral of success, Wilton Abbey experienced fluctuating fortunes during the thirteenth and fourteenth centuries: money for necessary repairs was not always easily found; the nuns were not always well-behaved. In 1539 the Abbey was reported to be in a 'ruinous' state. This, however, was exaggeration; it suited a government with evil intent to say so. Whilst it was true that Wilton had lost some of its earlier lustre, it remained the fourth largest convent in England. And whilst none could equal the fame of Edith, any abbess was, by default, always an important figure in the Wiltshire community, not only as a spiritual leader but as a landowner who exercised baronial and judicial rights.[1]

We know the names of 33 of Wilton's abbesses but often little more. Partial exceptions are the two women who would be the last in that long line. Isabel Jordayne, considered 'ancient, wise and discreet', and herself a Wilton nun, was the Abbey's favoured candidate to become Abbess when Cecilia Willoughby died on September 28th 1528. But what should have been a formality was complicated by a lady at Court whom Henry VIII was finding

1   Pugh & Crittall, *Wiltshire*, III, pp. 231-42.

increasingly attractive: Ann Boleyn. Ann lobbied the claims of
Eleanor Carey, her brother-in-law's sister. Although Jordayne
prevailed, it was an inauspicious beginning. She struggled to exert
her authority: her problems were compounded, first by an outbreak
of plague, and then by a dormitory fire.

Jordayne may well have been put on the early modern equivalent
of gardening leave before her death in 1534.[1] Her successor was
Celia Bodenham. Evidently an astute operator with connections
(she was known both to Henry VIII and his new wife, now
Queen Ann Boleyn), Celia ensured a smooth passage to Wilton
by paying £100 to the King's Secretary, Thomas Cromwell. But
neither connections nor money could help her turn the tide that
was about to engulf monasticism. Wilton was not amongst the
smaller religious houses dissolved by the Crown in 1536, but when
the King sought richer pickings Celia offered little resistance. She
surrendered the Abbey, herself and 33 nuns to Henry on March
25th 1539. 'Methinks', wrote one of the nuns, 'that the Abbess hath
a faint heart and doth yield up our possessions to the spoiler with a
not unwilling haste'.[2] A pension of £100 (the Abbey was valued at
£700), a farm at nearby Fovant, and the continued services of at least
ten nuns, helped ease whatever pain her decision had caused her.

A broadly similar sequence of events was unfolding across the
land. By 1540 Henry VIII had an enormous windfall of assets at
his disposal. Some he kept, some he sold, and some he gifted away.
Wilton Abbey and its estate, in excess of 40,000 acres, would fall
into the latter category. First, in 1541, the King issued a grant to
'William Herbert, Esquire and Anne his wife for the term of their
lives'. Three years later, he extended his generosity in a second grant
'to the aforementioned lord, by the name of Sir William Herbert,
Knight, and the Lady Anne his wife and heirs male of their bodies
between them lawfully begotten'.[3] The story of the Herberts at
Wilton House had begun.

1   *ODNB*, 'Isabel Jordayne'.
2   https://en.wikipedia.org/wiki/Cecily_Bodenham, accessed 29 Mar.
2022.
3   Robinson, *Wilton House*, p. 31.

Part 1
Founding Females c. 1551-1857

ANNE PARR

ANNE PARR (1515-1552) was the youngest child of a leading Westmorland family, the Parrs of Kendal. Her father, Sir Thomas Parr, was married to Maud Green of Northamptonshire stock. Unfortunately for her historical reputation, Anne has been overshadowed by her elder siblings, Catherine, sixth wife of Henry VIII, and William, who became 1st Marquess of Northampton in 1559. But whereas they had no surviving issue, Anne had three children, all of whom reached adulthood. Her descendants thrive at Wilton to this day.

Although born of non-aristocratic standing, Anne could boast several royal ties. Her paternal grandmother, Elizabeth Fitzhugh, was descended from John of Gaunt, Duke of Lancaster. Fitzhugh was also a niece of Richard Neville (Warwick the 'Kingmaker'), and became a lady in waiting to her cousin, Anne Neville, consort of Richard III. Through her second marriage to Nicholas Vaux, 1st Lord Harowden, Elizabeth Fitzhugh could also claim connection with Lady Margaret Beaufort, mother of Henry VII.

Anne's father, Sir Thomas Parr, was one of many who seem to have fallen foul of the notorious rapacity of Henry VII. In any event, the young Henry VIII cancelled his debt of £9,000 and granted him an annuity of 50 marks. Sir Thomas went on to enjoy considerable favour from Henry: he became variously Master of the Wards, Comptroller of the Household, and Master of the Guards.

2. Anne Parr by Hans Holbein the Younger, c. 1530

Additional proof of the King's esteem was his being entrusted to hold the canopy over the Princess Mary, Henry's firstborn, at her christening in 1516. He was also despatched to accompany Margaret, Henry's elder sister, Queen Dowager of Scotland, on her visit to England in 1516. According to the sixteenth century scholar, Roger Ascham, Sir Thomas was, to boot, a most charming man. He died of sweating sickness in 1517.[1]

1   D. Starkey, *Six Wives. The Queens of Henry VIII*, pp. 690-3.

In 1507 Sir Thomas purchased the wardship of Maud Green; he married her in 1508.[1] Maud was descended from Sir Henry Green, a distinguished Lord Chief Justice during the reign of Edward III. She was confident and intelligent, loved learning and was fluent in French. A maid to Catherine of Aragon, Henry VIII's first queen, Lady Maud seems to have had a special responsibility for the royal nursery. Lord Dacre, for one, was anxious for his grandson, Henry Scrope, to go there in 1523 that 'he might learn with her as well as any place that I know, as well as nurture in French and other languages'. Maud's name can be found in the royal accounts as being entitled to breakfast at the Crown's expense, and with suits of livery to be provided for her servants and their lodging when in the Queen's service. She accompanied Queen Catherine to France in 1520 for the famous summit meeting between Henry VIII and Francis I, near Calais, known as the Field of Cloth of Gold. She was wealthy enough in her own right, as co-heiress of lands in eight counties, that she was assessed for 1,000 marks in 1522. Mary I (1516-1558) would remember her with affection.

Anne too, would be imbued with a love of learning. Her mother, Maud, taught her to read and write as a young child; she played chess with her siblings. It seems likely that she would also have attended the royal nursey of which her mother was erstwhile head. If so, she would have mixed with the Princess Mary, only a few months her junior, and been tutored by the renowned Spanish scholar Juan Lluis Vives. The enlightened curriculum would have included theology, philosophy, French and the Classics; she also developed what became lifelong interests in art and music. Roger Ascham, writing of Anne during the 1540s, declared her to be an 'accomplished scholar'. As the following snippet makes clear, he both praised and encouraged her study of Latin: 'At last I send you your Cicero, most noble lady; since you are delighted so

---

1　Maud's father, accused of treason, had died in the Tower of London when she was a minor. As such, she became a ward of the Crown. Selling wardships was a lucrative source of revenue; the Master of the Wards, in consequence, was a much coveted office.

much by his books, you do wisely to study them. You will study most diligently and not need any exhortation'.[1]

Soon after her mother died, probably in 1531, Anne entered royal service as a maid of honour to Catherine of Aragon. Her position in life looked secure. Sir Thomas had left 400 marks in his will for 'her entertainment and marriage'. To this, her mother's will added a share in plate worth a further 400 marks and a third of her jewels, 'in coffers locked in with divers locks, whereof every one of them my executors and my daughter Anne to have every one of them a key ... and there it to remain till it ought to be delivered unto her'. She seems also to have been bequeathed the lease of a farm in Essex, but this, despite Anne's brother's protestations, was seized by the acquisitive Thomas Cromwell in 1533.[2]

Anne prospered as Cromwell ultimately would not. When Catherine of Aragon's marriage to the King was annulled, Anne was kept on as a maid of honour to Ann Boleyn, Queen from June 1533. The new Queen, highly educated, was an advocate of the new learning in religion which, a generation later, would evolve into Protestantism. Whether she encountered a kindred spirit in the maid of honour fifteen years her junior we shall never know. A tantalising hypothesis suggests that she might have. When Ann Boleyn went to the block in May 1536 she was supported by four young, but unnamed, ladies who were left with the gruesome task of finding a coffin – an arrow chest had to suffice – for her corpse. Might Anne Parr have been amongst their number? Even if she was not, we do know that she retained her position as maid of honour to Jane Seymour, who married the King only hours after Ann Boleyn's execution. Eighteen months later, following Jane's death twelve days after giving birth to the future Edward VI, Anne Parr was numbered amongst her funeral cortege, 'Mris [sic] Parre', riding in the fourth carriage. She also attended the young

1   A. Nicolson, *Earls of Paradise*, pp. 53-57; A. Martienssen, *Queen Catherine Parr*, p. 21. Vives (1493-1540) is sometimes described as the father of modern psychology.
2   Starkey, *Six Wives*, p. 709.

Prince's baptism on October 15th 1537 on which occasion she may have carried the train of the four year old Princess Elizabeth. In 1540 she was promoted to be Chief Gentlewoman of the Privy Chamber when Anne of Cleves became Henry VIII's fourth wife.[1]

Henry was between wives when Anne Parr herself married. We do not know the precise date but she is possibly the woman being referred to when John Husee told Lady Lisle, in August 1537, that 'it is thought Mrs Parre will shortly marry'.[2] Her intended was William Herbert. Born in 1506, Herbert was a grandson of the Welsh magnate William Herbert, Earl of Pembroke. He was not quite so great a match for Anne as that fact suggests: the title had been extinguished when Pembroke was executed for treason in 1469; the younger William's father, moreover, was only an illegitimate son of the deceased. Hot tempered, 'tall, strong set but bony', his future had seemed decidedly problematic when he killed a man in a brawl in Bristol in 1527, but a brief spell abroad fighting in the service of Francis I, allowed him to escape formal justice. He was certainly a member of the royal household by 1531; in 1535 he was appointed an esquire of the King's body, one of a select band of personal attendants, clearly popular and trusted, and on an upward career spiral. The general consensus is that he and Anne married some time in 1538. There is nothing to suggest that it was not a love match.[3]

Anne and William's marriage appears also to have catalysed their good fortune. William became a Gentleman of the Privy Chamber in 1540; Anne, who received 50 shillings from the King in 1539, became a Gentlewoman of the Privy Chamber to the Queen (from July 1540, Catherine Howard) at about the same time. Anne was given special responsibility for the Queen's jewels, overseeing their transfer from, and safe return to, the

1　Starkey, *Six Wives*, p. 709.
2　*ODNB*, 'William Herbert, 1st Earl of Pembroke'.
3　*ODNB*, 'William Herbert, 1st Earl of Pembroke'; S.J. Gunn & W.R.B. Robinson, 'The Early Life of William Herbert, earl of Pembroke (d. 1570)', *Welsh History Review*, XVIII (1996-7), pp. 509-19.

Queen's wardrobe in Baynard's Castle at Blackfriars.[1] The chief manifestations of the couple's success, however, were the birth of a son, Henry, in 1539, and the lifetime grant of the Wilton estate in 1541.[2] Not the least remarkable detail in that document was the fact of the grant's being made jointly to Anne and William, not just William, as one might have expected to have been the case in such a patriarchical world.

Catherine Howard, guilty of adultery, fell spectacularly from grace in November 1541. Anne not only survived the resulting scandal that engulfed several of her contemporaries but was trusted by the King to accompany Catherine to Syon House in Middlesex pending her trial. Following Catherine's execution, in April 1542, Anne was released from her duties, by the 'special gift and confidence that we have held in our dere and best beloved, Anne Herbert, wife of our trusty servant William Herbert Esq ... one of the Gentlewomen of the Privy Chamber ...' But she was evidently back in some form of royal service a few months later: John Dudley, writing to Anne's brother, William, informed him early in 1543 'that ... your sister and Mrs Herbert be both here at Court with my Lady Mary's Grace, and my Lady Elizabeth'.[3]

The sister alluded to, of course, was Catherine Parr. Herself twice widowed, she became the sixth wife of Henry VIII when she married him on July 12th 1543. Anne and William were amongst the twenty or so guests at the wedding which was held in the Queen's Privy Closet at Hampton Court; the ensuing family celebrations were perhaps the occasion for their elevation to the status of Sir William and Lady Herbert.[4] They were certainly styled as that in the grant of 1544 which gifted them the Wilton estate in perpetuity. Given the timing, it is inconceivable that the grant was anything other than the consequence of Anne's having become Henry VIII's sister-in-law.

1   Martienssen, *Catherine Parr*, p. 137.
2   *ODNB*, 'William Herbert, 1st Earl of Pembroke'.
3   Starkey, *Six Wives*, p. 713. Henry VIII's daughters, then aged 16 and 9 respectively, later Mary I and Elizabeth 1.
4   Starkey, *Six Wives*, pp. 713-14.

Nor is it surprising to learn that by the end of 1544 Anne had been promoted to become the Chief Lady of the Queen's Privy Chamber, 'the dominant force in the Queen's Household'.[1] She assisted her sister, the Queen, at the traditional Maundy Thursday ritual of washing the feet of a group of poor women in April 1544. Lady Anne was dressed, at Catherine's behest, in a 'black double jean velvet outfit': the King likened her appearance to that of a crow. Queen Catherine also gifted part of Baynard's Castle (near the present day St Paul's Cathedral) to the Herberts to use as a London residence. It remained the family's main home in the capital until destroyed in the Great Fire of London of 1666.

Anne must surely have found this period of her life especially enjoyable. High status and a happy family life combined with a regime in the privy chamber which focused on learning. John Foxe, the sixteenth century martyrologist, claimed that 'every day in the afternoon, for the space of an hour, one of her [Queen Catherine] said chaplains in her privy chamber, made some collation to her and her ladies and gentlemen of her privy chamber, or others that were disposed to hear; in which sermons they oftimes touched upon such abuses as in the church then were rife'. Lady Anne must have revelled in the opportunities such a forum provided for intellectual stimulation and debate. We know that she gifted a book, covered in silver and gilt, worth 7s 6d, to Princess Mary in 1544. She was also a patron of scholars such as John Pindar and Reginald Middleton, of St John's College, Cambridge.

There was, however, one dangerous episode, which occurred in March 1546, which cannot be overlooked. To discuss religion in the latter years of Henry VIII's reign was literally – given that the punishment for heresy was burning – playing with fire. The official line, from 1539, was that England was essentially theologically Catholic. Queen Catherine and Lady Anne (Sir William too) undoubtedly inclined by now to see the nation move in a more Protestant direction. Mindful that Catherine was lobbying the King to this end, religious conservatives,

---

1   Starkey, *Six Wives*, p. 748.

spearheaded by Stephen Gardiner, the Bishop of Winchester, sought to persuade Henry that she held heretical opinions. According to John Foxe, 'to ascertain what books forbidden by law she had in her closet … they thought it best, at first, to begin with some of those ladies, whom they knew to be great with her, and of her blood; the chiefest whereof, as most of estimation and privy to all her doings were these: the lady Herbert, afterward countess of Pembroke, and sister to the queen, and chief of her privy chamber … upon their apprehension in the court, their closets and coffers should have been searched, that somewhat might have been found by which the Queen might be charged; which being found, the queen herself should have been taken, and likewise carried by night by barge to the Tower'.[1] The King seems to have given his permission for some sort of search to take place. Catherine, however, got wind of what was afoot and, taking Anne with her, abased herself sufficiently before him that he forgave any transgressions, real or otherwise. Lord Chancellor Wriothesley, unaware of this development, had just reached Whitehall with 40 men to escort Lady Anne and the others to the Tower when the news reached him. For Lady Anne, well aware of her brother-in-law's capricious nature, Wriothesley's appearance must have thrown her into a state of terror.[2]

Either shortly before or shortly after this, Anne retired to her sister's manor at Hanworth, near Twickenham, where she gave birth to a second son, Edward. Queen Catherine paid for 'five yeomen and two grooms riding to Hanworthe at the [christe]ning of the Lady Herbertes child'.[3] Henry VIII died in January 1547. We next hear of Anne, in May 1547, in a letter written to Catherine at her Chelsea lodgings by Thomas Seymour. The latter was a key member of the Regency Council (Sir William was also a member) set up to govern England whilst Edward VI (b. 1537) was a minor. After supper at Baynard's Castle, Lady

---

1   *ODNB*, 'Anne Parr'. The other women targeted were Lady Maud Lane, a cousin of the Parr sisters, and Lady Elizabeth Tyrwhit.
2   J.J. Scarisbrick, *Henry VIII*, pp. 478-81.
3   S. James, *Catherine Parr*, pp. 275-6.

Anne 'had waded further with me touching my lodging with your Highness at Chelsea, which I denied, but that indeed I went by the garden as I went to the Bishop of London's house, and at this point stood with her a long time, till at last she told me by further tokens, which made me change colour, who like a false wench, took me with the manner, then remembering what she was, and knowing how well ye trusted her'.[1]

Thomas Seymour's embarrassment was the consequence of Lady Anne's knowledge of his secret dalliance with the Queen Dowager. Both Lady Anne and Sir William were present for the marriage a few weeks later. It did not end well: Catherine died in childbirth in September 1548; the ambitious, but impolitic, Seymour was beheaded in March 1549. The more canny Herberts, by contrast, were soon to reach the apogee of their good fortune together. At some point during 1550, Lady Anne gave birth to her third child, a daughter, also named Anne. Then, on October 11th 1551, as part of the carve up by which leading members of the Regency Council deemed it fit to reward themselves, Sir William and Lady Anne became the 1st Earl and Countess of Pembroke of the tenth creation.[2]

Anne's life had given her good cause to know that fortune is fickle. She died suddenly at Baynard's Castle, on February 20th 1552, aged only 36. Although the cause of her death is not known, there is an account of her lavish funeral from the diary of Londoner Henry Machin: 'On 28 February was buried the noble Countess of Pembroke, sister to the late queen Katheryn, wife of Henry VIII. She died at Baynard's Castle, and was carried into St Paul's. There were 100 poor men and women who had mantle frieze gowns. Then came heralds; after this the corpse, and about her, eight banner roll of arms. Then came the mourners, both lords and knights and gentlemen, also the lady and gentlewomen mourners to the number of 200. After these were 200 of her own and other servants in coats. She was buried by the tomb of

---

1   T. Lever, *The Herberts of Wilton*, pp. 7-8.
2   Ann Boleyn was granted the title Marchioness of Pembroke in 1532. It lapsed with her execution in 1536.

Lancaster [John of Gaunt]. Afterwards her banners were set up over her, and her arms set on divers pillars'.[1]

The Earl inscribed her memorial 'a most faithful wife, a woman of the greatest piety and discretion'. For all its sycophancy, a more revealing epitaph was provided by William Thomas, Clerk of Edward VI's Privy Council. Thomas dedicated *The Vanitee of the World* to Lady Anne in 1549:

> To the right worshipful and my singular good Lady, the Lady Anne Herbert of Wilton ... because I have found so much negligence in man, that almost he desireth not to be warned any more of his folly: therefore did I determine to dedicate my boke unto a woman, to prove whether it may take any root in them: to the extent that men ashamed, through the virtuous examples of women, may be provoked thereby to reform themselves, which no kind admission can persuade them to do. And finding amongst women your ladyship in virtue and bounty to excel as the diamond amongst the jewels, I thought it my duty to commend it specially unto you. Assuring myself, that the wonderful qualities and modesty of your Ladyship shall be a noblesse terror to them.[2]

Anne Parr was Countess of Pembroke for a shorter time than any of her successors. Henry, her eldest son, lived to become 2nd Earl, but she was dead before he became a teenager. Neither did she live to see the splendour of the great house that her husband created at Wilton. Without her, given William Herbert's shrewd instincts and good fortune, there may well still have been Earls of Pembroke. Because of Anne, however, and through her sister, the Pembroke estate was larger than it would otherwise have been. Overshadowed by both husband and sister, Anne was a more important figure in her own right than history has allowed. All Earls and Countesses of Pembroke stand in her debt.

1   Nicholson, *Earls of Paradise*, pp. 72-73.
2   Quotation modernised.

Lady Ann Talbot

The first Earl remarried in the late spring of 1552. His new Countess was Lady Ann Talbot, a daughter of George, 4th Earl of Shrewsbury.[1] She would be married to Pembroke (and thus Countess) for eighteen years. It was during her time, though there is no evidence that she played any part in the design, that Wilton Abbey was recast to create a grand Tudor house. Its four ranges with corner towers around an inner court were suggestive as much of the old convent as a new castle. Most of the work was probably planned, if not executed, during the reign of Edward VI. We know that the young King came to Wilton, where he was 'wondrously entertained', in 1552.[2] Progress was interrupted during the reign of Mary Tudor (1553-1558) when legislation paved the way for the revival of monasticism. Legend has it that

3. The Tudor East front, Wilton House, c. 1565

1   From Shrewsbury's second marriage to Elizabeth Walden. Ann was widow of Peter Compton.
2   J.M. Robinson, *Wilton House*, pp. 29, 45-6, 56, 59.

the Earl welcomed the returning nuns with an admission of his sinfulness only to reveal his true colours when Elizabeth's accession signalled the final death of English monasticism: 'like a tygre', he unceremoniously showed them the door with a valedictory 'Out ye whores, to worke, to worke, ye whores, goe spinne'.[1] But we know nothing about his relations with his second wife other than that they were childless and that she complained to Queen Elizabeth that he had overlooked her in his will. One can reasonably infer from this that Pembroke set greater store by his first marriage of thirteen years to Anne Parr than his second marriage of eighteen years to Ann Talbot. It was Anne Parr alongside whom he would be laid when he died in 1570. A magnificent new tomb was raised over them.[2]

1   A. Clark (ed), *John Aubrey's Brief Lives*, I, p. 316.
2   The old St Paul's, like Baynard's Castle, perished in the Great Fire of 1666.

LADY CATHERINE GREY

S TILL VERY MUCH alive at mid-century, the 1st Earl was the *éminence grise* behind the most audacious Herbert marriage ever to have taken place. Edward VI and his council, of which Pembroke remained a prominent member, had piloted a Protestant church settlement through Parliament in 1552. By June 1553, however, it was clear that Edward VI was dying of 'consumption' (probably pulmonary tuberculosis). Since Mary Tudor, his half-sister and legal heir, was a devout Catholic, both Protestantism and those who had championed it, were in jeopardy.[1] Protestants needed a plan. The King, the Duke of Northumberland, but surely also Pembroke, reasoned that the succession might be varied, specifically that the throne should by-pass Henry VIII's children on the grounds of their alleged illegitimacy, and pass instead to the heirs of Henry VIII's sister, Mary Tudor (she of *Mary Rose* fame). First in line was her granddaughter, Lady Jane Grey. Should she fail to produce male heirs, the throne would pass to her younger sister Catherine.[2]

Catherine Grey was born on August 25th 1540. It may well be that Pembroke envisaged her as his eldest son's bride before the events outlined above unfolded. There is some suggestion that Catherine and Henry Herbert were betrothed during the summer of 1552 when both were around twelve years old. No doubt exists, however, that they were married on May 21st 1553 at Durham House in London before taking up residence at Baynard's Castle. By a less than strange coincidence, Catherine's sister, Lady Jane, married Northumberland's son, Lord Guildford Dudley, the same day.

1 Edward's other half-sister, Elizabeth, kept her religious cards close to her chest; there were plenty who doubted her legitimacy.
2 P. Williams, *The Later Tudors*, pp. 82-85.

Having drawn up his 'Devise' for the succession, endorsed by his council in June, Edward VI died on July 6th. Pembroke was amongst the first to kneel and kiss the hands of the new Queen Jane. Thirteen days later, as it became clear that the political nation viewed the 'Devise' as a coup, and that the throne rightly belonged to Henry VIII's daughter, Mary Tudor, Pembroke threw a purse of gold coins to the crowd and declared for Mary. He also sought a rapid annulment of Catherine and Henry's marriage on the grounds of non-consummation. Northumberland, Catherine's sister, Jane, and her young husband, Lord Guildford Dudley, were all executed; Pembroke lived to be present at Mary's coronation. Perhaps Queen Mary's former regard for Anne Parr and William Herbert played a part in saving the latter's neck?

4. *Monument of Lady Catherine Grey and Lord Hertford, Salisbury Cathedral (Wikimedia Commons)*

With Elizabeth succeeding 'Bloody' Mary on the throne in November 1558, reluctant to marry and unwilling to name an heir, Catherine gained a renewed prominence. The ever-ambitious Pembroke mooted reviving Catherine's marriage with his son,

Henry, Lord Herbert.[1] Elizabeth was furious when Catherine did indeed marry for a second time. But Lord Herbert was not the husband. Rather, it was Edward Seymour, 1st Earl of Hertford, nephew of Henry VIII's third wife. They married secretly in December 1560. Elizabeth had them consigned to The Tower, but evidently not in separate confinement, since Catherine had given birth to two sons by 1562. Archbishop Matthew Parker annulled the marriage the same year. Catherine was censured for 'carnal copulation', released from The Tower, and then placed under virtual house arrest from 1563 until her death from consumption on January 26th 1568.[2]

Catherine lies buried today with her second husband, Lord Hertford, in Salisbury Cathedral. On their monument, her effigy, befitting her royal status, is raised a few inches higher than his. Ironically, the monument is just a few yards from her first husband's final resting place in the Herbert family vault.

1   Lever, *Herberts of Wilton*, pp. 30-32.
2   Williams, *The Later Tudors*, p. 243.

LADY KATHERINE TALBOT

Henry, Lord Herbert's second marriage may have been determined in part by his stepmother, Ann Talbot, though the Herberts needed little prompting to further their ties with one of the great governing families. At all events there was a double marriage in 1562: Henry, Lord Herbert, married Katherine Talbot, daughter of George Talbot, 6th Earl of Shrewsbury, whilst Lady Anne Herbert, his sister (daughter of Anne Parr and the 1st Earl of Pembroke) married Lord Francis Talbot. The marriages seem to have been happy enough but they were not long. Anne died before she could become Countess of Shrewsbury; Katherine, Lady Pembroke, died in 1576, just six years after she became Countess of Pembroke, and only two years after Queen Elizabeth spent three nights at Wilton in September 1574. Katherine had been one of her favourites: the Queen visited her twice during her final illness at Baynard's Castle.[1]

1   Lever, *Herberts of Wilton*, pp. 32, 36-7.

MARY SIDNEY

MARY SIDNEY was born on October 27th 1561 at Tickenhall in Worcestershire. She was one of the three surviving children (at least four siblings died) of Sir Henry Sidney and Mary Dudley. Her maternal grandfather was John Dudley, Duke of Northumberland, the central figure in the failed plot to put Lady Jane Grey on the throne in 1553. The Dudleys were sufficiently close to the Herberts that William, 1st Earl of Pembroke, had agreed to stand as one of Mary Sidney's godparents.[1]

Contemporary biographer and antiquarian John Aubrey tells us that Mary was attractive with 'a pretty sharpe-ovall face. Her haire was of a reddish yellowe.'[2] We can reasonably infer that she was schooled in Classics and modern languages. Mary also displayed an aptitude for music: her greatest proficiency lay in playing the lute, though she was also praised for her singing. She was also adept in needlework. Examples of her work sat alongside the tapestries displayed at Wilton. As the poet John Taylor quipped, Mary was both 'A Patterne and a Patronesse'.[3]

There is, however, no explicit reference to Mary Sidney before February 1575. It appears in a letter from Queen Elizabeth I to Mary's father, then serving her in Ireland. In condoling with him on the death of his daughter, Ambrosia, the Queen urged Sir Henry to find solace in 'ye comfort of one daughter [Mary] of very good hope'. From a practical point of view Elizabeth added that 'if ye should think good to remoue from those parts of unpleasant ayre (if it be so) into better in these partes, and will send her unto us before Easter, or when you shall think good, assure yourself that we will haue a speciall care of her'. This was sensible: Mary's

---

1   F.B. Young, *Mary Sidney*, ch. 1, *passim*.
2   Clark, *John Aubrey's Brief Lives*, I, p. 311.
3   Nicolson, *Earls of Paradise*, pp. 100-102.

mother, evidently close to the monarch, was a Gentlewoman of the Privy Chamber.[1]

Young Mary soon came to the attention of the recently widowed Henry, 2nd Earl of Pembroke, by now a powerful figure at Court. But it was her uncle, Robert Dudley, Earl of Leicester, a great favourite with the Queen, who was the chief architect of their match. The fact that the Earl was well over twenty years Mary's senior was not especially unusual, nor the fact that she was only fifteen when their marriage was agreed. Her father thought the substantial dowry of £3,000 well worth the paying. Pembroke's receipt for £1,000 of the dowry still exists. Mary married him on April 21st 1577.[2] We do not know what her thoughts were as a pawn in the marriage game but few, if any, believe that hers was a love match. The Earl has not enjoyed a good press. None of his number has been more overshadowed by his own wife; few have had to endure so overbearing a father. John Aubrey claimed that the 1st Earl was so convinced of his son's charmlessness that Mary, 'his faire and witty daughter-in-lawe would horne his sonne … and advised him to keep her in the Countrey and not to let her frequent the Court.'[3] There is, in fact, no suggestion that Mary was ever unfaithful. Even the scurrilous Aubrey dismissed talk that the 4th Earl was the lovechild of Mary and her brother Philip, if only because he 'inherited not the witt of either'. Mary's husband, however, was conspicuous for his lack of tact and contrived, despite Mary's emollience, to alienate many. Beset by ill health, he cannot have been an easy man with whom to live.[4]

Mary took some comfort, if such were needed, in her new surroundings. She spent much of her early married life at Wilton, and also at the Herbert family's Wiltshire properties of Ramsbury

1   Young, *Mary Sidney*, pp. 27-28.
2   *ODNB*, 'Mary Sidney'.
3   This was patently untrue: the Earl had died in 1570.
4   Clark, *John Aubrey's Brief Lives*, I, pp. 310-11; *ODNB*, 'Henry, 2nd Earl of Pembroke'. Since the 1st Earl had died in 1570, Aubrey was, at the very least, misattributing his source.

5. Mary Sidney, engraving by B. Reading, after S. Van der Passe (Wikimedia Commons)

Manor and Ivychurch in Alderbury. The latter, in particular, only seven miles east of Wilton, 'much delighted her'.[1] So did visits from members of her family, none more so than those by her brother, Philip.

Seven years older than Mary, Philip Sidney was one of the 'superstars' of Elizabethan England. Handsome, intelligent, diplomat and soldier, Philip's zest for humanist learning fused with a personal charisma which made him the chief focus of a literary circle which included the writer and politician, Fulke Greville, and the poet Edmund Spenser. But it was Mary who was the focus of Philip's attentions when he paid an extended visit to Wiltshire during the spring and summer of 1580. Before he left, he had begun the work known today as *The Countess of Pembroke's Arcadia*. 'You desired me to doe it', the preface proclaimed, 'and your desire to my heart is an absolute commandment'. It was written 'in loose sheetes of paper, most of it in your presence, the rest, by sheetes, sent unto you, as fast as they were done'.[2] Tradition has it that Philip received some of the inspiration for his verse whilst walking along a path across the River Nadder on the south side of Wilton Park. Mary is reputed to have laid out

1   S. Lee, 'Mary Sidney', *Dictionary of National Biography*, XXVI, pp. 205-7.
2   Nicolson, *Earls of Paradise*, p. 114.

what today is known as Sir Philip Sidney's Walk in his memory. The connection was underscored further in the series of 26 painted scenes from *Arcadia* which adorn the dado of the Single Cube Room in the mid-seventeenth century State Apartment commissioned by his nephew, Philip, 4th Earl of Pembroke.[1]

Sir Philip (he was knighted in 1583) was as zealous for Protestantism as he was for learning. Hence his enthusiasm for Dutch rebels in their struggle for independence against Catholic Spain, the alacrity with which he accepted appointment as Governor of Flushing in 1585, and his readiness to risk his life in the cause. He paid the ultimate price when he died in Arnhem, on October 17th 1586, from wounds sustained besieging Zutphen a month previously. For Mary it was an *annus horribilis*: her father died in May, her mother in August. She seems to have entered a period of prolonged grief. At any event, Mary does not re-emerge into the public record until 1588. She would do so in spectacular fashion.[2]

Mary's three claims on posterity overlap: as her brother's chief literary custodian, as the patron of a famed literary salon, and as a writer of consequence in her own right. To her, it was the first that mattered most. She was never prouder than when referring to herself as 'Sidney's sister'. An important example was to see his 1580 essay, *An Apology for Poetry*, through the press in 1595. By then Mary had devoted herself to completing Sir Philip's 'half-maim'd peece', a translation of the Psalms. As she put it, 'Hee did warpe, I weav'd this web to end'. Her end, although *The Sidney Psalms* would not be published until 1823, was to create 'a world of words'.[3]

Mary's most pressing endeavour, however, was to formalise *Arcadia*. Parts of it had been circulated (a not unusual practice) during the 1580s. An unauthorised version, in three books, the

---

1 Robinson, *Wilton House*, pp. 63, 99. *Arcadia* was composed nearly two centuries before the creation of the naturalised landscape which greets today's visitor to Wilton.
2 *ODNB*, 'Mary Sidney'.
3 Nicolson, *Earls of Paradise*, p. 125.

catalyst for Mary's involvement, had been published in 1590. Mary reshaped the whole by sub-dividing it into five parts, adding material from manuscripts in her possession, and inserting some material of her own composition. It was, she stated in the preface to her 1593 edition of *Arcadia*, the product of 'her honourable labour ... in correcting the faults ... [and] ended in supplying the defects'. A further edition was published in 1598, and included an appendix of some of Sir Philip's poems.[1]

John Aubrey famously described Mary as 'the greatest Patroness of witt and learning of any Lady in her time'. His claim can be quantified. There are at least twenty five known works dedicated to Mary by no fewer than eighteen different authors. Mary was 'the first non-royal woman in England to receive a significant number of dedications.' The most extravagant examples include Abraham Fraunce's *The Countesse of Pembrokes Ivychurch*, and Nicholas Breton's *The Countess of Pembrokes Passion*. T.S. Eliot's explanation for such obvious sycophancy was that Mary must have exercised a measure of formal control over a circle of writers at Wilton working in pursuit of her literary ideals.[2]

Some writers, however, were genuinely inspired by Mary. The poet Samuel Daniel, for example, happily admitted that he had received 'the first notion for the formall ordering of those compositions at Wilton, which I must ever acknowledge to have beene my best Schoole'. Equally, Mary did sometimes direct writers. Daniel was one such. His *Tragedie of Cleopatra* was a 'worke the which she did impose'.[3] Recent research, however, provides us with a more nuanced understanding of the nature of patronage. Some writers offered dedications in the hope of financial reward; some looked for protection from the censors. More commonly,

1   Lee, 'Mary Sidney', p. 205.
2   Clark, *John Aubrey's Brief Lives*, I, p. 311; M. Lamb, 'The Countess of Pembroke's Patronage', *English Literary Renaissance*, XII (1982), p. 163; *ODNB*, 'Mary Sidney'.
3   *ODNB*, 'Mary Sidney'; Lamb, 'The Countess of Pembroke's Patronage', p. 167.

writers were interested in personal advancement, or indeed a position of any sort. Mary's husband was, after all, a powerful man at Court: writing in homage to Mary could be a vehicle for influencing Earl Henry.[1]

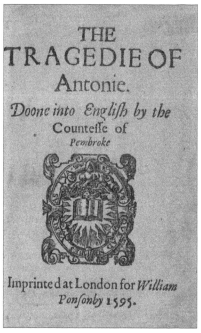

Mary's Wilton Circle was consequently less numerous and illustrious than is popularly remembered. They were nine in number. Four had been friends of Sir Philip: Abraham Fraunce, Nicholas Breton, Nathaniel Baxter and Edmund Spenser. The other five were people who had a more practical association with Wilton.

6. Title page from the Countess of Pembroke's The Tragedie of Antonie, 1595 (Wikimedia Commons)

They were Hugh Sanford, tutor and secretary, the Reverend Gervase Babington, family chaplain, Dr Thomas Muffet, family physician, Samuel Daniel, children's tutor, and Thomas Howell, an old family retainer. The extraordinary talents of playwright, Ben Jonson, and the metaphysical poet, John Donne, are more strongly associated with Wilton through the patronage of Mary's son, William 3rd Earl of Pembroke. And Shakespeare, though he is commemorated by a grand statue inside Wilton's front entrance today, was likely to have been a visitor but never an habitué.[2]

One should perhaps downplay the idea of Mary as patron and emphasise instead the notion of Mary's Wilton as a college.

1   Lamb, 'The Countess of Pembroke's Patronage', pp. 162-79.
2   Lamb, 'The Countess of Pembroke's Patronage', pp. 166-7.

The poet Nicholas Breton, who experienced it first hand, wrote of Wilton 'being in a maner a kind of little Court ... her person no less than worthily and honourablie attended, as well with Gentlewomen of excellent spirits, as diurers Gentlemen of fine carriage ... God daily serued, religion trulie preached, a table fully furnished, a house richly garnished, honor kindly entertained, virtue highly esteemed, seruice highly rewarded, and the poor blessed relieved'.[1] In such an environment – Wilton also boasted a fine library of Mary's creation – writers could retreat, relax, find inspiration and exchange ideas. Mary herself, and this was unusual for a woman at that time, circulated her own work beyond members of the Wilton Circle for criticism.

College life at Wilton, moreover, catered for more than writers: Mary was interested in science. Aubrey tells us that 'she was a great Chymist, and spent yearly a great deal in that study'. Wilton seems to have housed a laboratory of sorts, the chief practitioner in which was Adrian Gilbert, a wealthy half-brother of Sir Walter Raleigh. Bemused contemporaries clearly discerned in Gilbert, ostensibly employed as a garden designer, the hallmarks of what we would now call a mad scientist. Aubrey called him 'the greatest Buffon in the Nation; cared not what he said to man or woman of what quality soever'. And straddling the arts-science divide, like Mary herself, was the curious figure of Dr Thomas Muffet. A world authority on the silkworm, he wrote a 42 page poem in 1599 entitled *The Silkewormes and their Flies*. Muffet's chief focus thereafter shifted from silkworms to spiders; his daughter, Patience, may have been the inspiration for the rhyme 'Little Miss Muffet'. But Muffet was interested in the insect world in its entirety. His study, *The Theater of Insects*, was an important contribution to entomology.[2]

More as Vice-Chancellor than patron, therefore, Mary was the first woman to preside at a Wilton that was something more than a home since Celia Bodenham and her nuns were evicted

1   Nicolson, *Earls of Paradise*, p. 128.
2   J. Allen & C. Bennett, *Mary Sidney Herbert*, pp. 72-75; Nicolson, *Earls of Paradise*, pp. 129-30.

from the Abbey in 1539. Under her benign stewardship, and through the ethos which she imparted, Wilton became more renowned as a centre of learning than at any time since the twelfth century. Only St Edith can rival the memory of Mary Sidney.

Whilst Mary's importance as a literary patron has been downgraded in recent decades, there has been increased recognition of her significance as an author. That Mary was underappreciated was partly her fault: she was ambivalent about self-advertisement. Whether this was born of modesty (though she was clearly confident in her own ability), awareness that female writers were generally frowned upon, or a sisterly desire to keep the spotlight on her beloved brother, are matters for debate. A good example of the latter is her signing off her contribution to *The Sidney Psalms* as being 'By the sister of that incomparable Sidney'. In reality, the translation of the Psalms is now regarded as Mary Sidney's most important literary achievement. Working together, even if it was largely Sir Philip's work, they had only completed 43 of the 150 Psalms before Sir Philip's untimely death.[1] It fell to Mary to translate the remaining 107 on her own.

Mary's determination to see the project to fruition, and the challenges she faced in doing so, are best understood in the context of the Reformation. Until then, the only version of the Bible allowed by law in England was in Latin. Not until 1539 had Parliament legislated that the Bible (the Psalms formed part of the Old Testament) should be available in the vernacular. Archbishop Thomas Cranmer had subsequently incorporated versions of the Psalms in his prayer books of 1549 and 1552, essentially the same as were included in the English prayer book of 1559 which formed part of Queen Elizabeth's moderately Protestant church settlement. Mary was born just two years later. The Sidneys, enthusiastic in their Protestantism, could not help but find all this both new and exciting. What better way to spread God's Word than by making it more widely accessible, the more so if it could be done in more poetic language?

1   Allen & Bennett, *Mary Sidney Herbert*, ch. 7, *passim*.

In producing an alternative rendering, Mary drew upon her formidable scholarship. She would have used the prayer books, unauthorised translations of the Bible effected by William Tyndale and Miles Coverdale in the earlier sixteenth century, and other texts in French by Continental theologians. She may even have known enough Hebrew to utilise Hebrew versions of the Bible too. But above all, Mary employed her facility for poetic language. Consider the first two verses of Psalm 84 from the King James Bible:

> How amiable are thy tabernacles, O Lord of Hosts!
> My soul longeth, yea, even fainteth for the courts of the Lord:
> my heart and my flesh crieth out for the living God.

Mary's skill and imagination transform the lines into:

> How lovely is thy dwelling,
> Great God, to whom all greatness is belonging!
> To view thy courts, far, far from any telling
> My soul doth long, and pine with longing
> Unto the God that liveth,
> The God that all life giveth.

Mary's version, is simpler, more evangelistic, more musical and generally more pleasing. Even if the reader disagrees, this is at least an attempt to convey a faint scent of Mary's style. Those wanting to experience the full flavour of her oeuvre must turn elsewhere.[1] George Herbert, the devotional poet (her kinsman by marriage), and John Donne, are amongst the luminaries who patently did just that. The latter wrote of *The Sidney Psalms* that 'They shew us Ilanders our joy, our King, They tell us *why*, and teach us *how* to sing'. Samuel Daniel predicted that they would ensure her 'fresh in fame' when '*Wilton* lyes low levell'd with the ground'.[2]

1   Allen & Bennett, *Mary Sidney Herbert*, pp. 115-16.
2   *ODNB*, 'Mary Sidney'.

The Sidney Psalms, for all their beauty, did not appear in print until 1823. During Mary's lifetime they only circulated in manuscript form, of which, remarkably, eighteen copies still survive. Of Mary's poems that were published during her lifetime, two praised her brother. One, *To the Angel Spirit of the Most Excellent Sir Philip Sidney*, 'Inspired by thee, thy secret power impressed', was used as an introduction to her edition of *Arcadia*. The other, *The Doleful Lay of Clorinda* ('to whom shall I my case complain, That may compassion my impatient grief?'), appeared under the aegis of Edmund Spenser in 1595. Another piece that found consummation in print before Mary died was *A dialogue between two Shepherds* (1599). It was written for the Queen as a preface to a special edition of *The Sidney Psalms* to mark the monarch's return to Wilton for the first time in 25 years. The visit, sadly, was cancelled.[1]

Better known in Mary's day than her poetry were some of her translations. The Frenchman Philippe de Mornay's *A Discourse of Life and Death* was dated by Mary as having been completed at Wilton on May 13th 1590. It emphasised the importance of reason and public duty for those in positions of authority. First published in 1592, it enjoyed three reprints. The contemporary scholar, Gabriel Harvey, called it 'a restorative electuary of gems'.[2] Published alongside it was Mary's version of Robert Garnier's *Marc Antoine*. It was the first time that the legendary tale of Antony and Cleopatra had been dramatized in English and helped to popularise the dramatic device of the soliloquy. Shakespeare borrowed from it for his reworking of the story fifteen years later. Mary also translated Petrarch's *The Triumph of Death*, but like *The Sidney Psalms*, it was only circulated in manuscript during her lifetime.

The 2nd Earl, for all his shortcomings, was the mainstay of Mary's support during these years. He died on January 19th 1601. In a gossipy letter John Chamberlain, a Court official, reported

1   *ODNB*, 'Mary Sidney'. The poem was published in 1602.
2   Lee, 'Mary Sidney', p. 206.

that the couple had not enjoyed good relations in their final years, the main consequence of which was that Henry determined to leave her 'as bare as he could, and bestowing all on the young lord, even to her jewels.' This was far from true. Pembroke's will bequeathed Mary £3,000 in plate, jewels and other goods, plus the rental income from several other properties. His caveat was that the latter would end should she cease to be 'solo and unmaryed'.[1]

Mary never did remarry. She was probably at Wilton when James I visited in 1603, but until the middle of the 1610s she lived principally at Crosby Hall in Chelsea. In 1615, however, the King granted Mary a manorial estate in Bedfordshire. She took advantage of the gift and built Houghton House: James I visited her there in July 1621. Advancing years did not diminish her strength of character. She was active in seeing that her children married well; and unflinching in her pursuit of those she believed had wronged her. Mary also travelled abroad, chiefly to the spa towns of Europe 'where she conducted a literary salon, wrote, danced, played cards, took tobacco, shot pistols, and carried on a flirtation with her handsome and learned doctor, Matthew Lister'.[2] She died in London, from smallpox, on September 25th 1621. Following a funeral in St Paul's Cathedral she was buried with her husband in Salisbury Cathedral.

It is unlikely that much remains to be discovered about Mary Sidney's life. On the basis of what is known, the most salient development over the past century or so has been the rise in Mary's reputation. Until the late Victorian period she was viewed very much, in the words of William Browne's famous seventeenth century epitaph, as 'Sidney's sister, Pembroke's mother.' Sidney Lee, in his entry for the *Dictionary of National Biography*, published in 1897, whilst allowing that Mary's writing 'shows culture and literary feeling', judged that 'Lady Pembroke's verse has few poetic qualities'. She rated 'to higher advantage' as a patron. In her biography of 1912, Frances Young acknowledged

1   Lamb, 'The Countess of Pembroke's Patronage', p. 166; *ODNB*, 'Henry, 2nd Earl of Pembroke'.
2   *ODNB*, 'Mary Sidney'.

Mary as 'a fair poet and an excellent translator' but was adamant that her fame rested foursquare on being her brother's friend and sibling.[1] From the 1960s onwards, however, partly in response to the expansion of higher education and the rise of the women's rights movement, Mary has attracted considerable attention as a female writer. Interested readers can now turn to such recondite titles as 'Relational Antifeminism in Sidney's "Arcadia"' or 'The Politics of Translation and Gender in the Countess of Pembroke's "Antonie"'.[2] Thankfully, the fruits of such research have percolated into more accessible studies. Simon Adams, for example, in his entry for the revised *Oxford Dictionary of National Biography*, published in 2004, lauds Mary 'as one of the first significant women writers in English'. More than that, Mary, excepting only the Queen, was the most brilliant woman to adorn Elizabethan England.

Mary should be feted at Wilton, however, primarily for a different reason. Her greatest service to the Herberts was to bear two sons who would carry forward the Pembroke dynasty. The 2nd Earl was in his forties by the time that William, his and Mary's first son, was born in 1580. Philip followed in 1584. They became successively the 3rd and 4th Earls. Without Mary, therefore, the earldom would have perished in just half a century. In the four centuries since her death, only one other Countess has matched her achievement of being mother to two Earls of Pembroke.[3]

1   Young, *Mary Sidney*, pp. 1, 23.
2   Allen & Bennett, *Mary Sidney Herbert*, pp. 181-6 for a bibliography.
3   There were at least two daughters: Katherine (1581-1584) and Anne (1583-1605?) who died unmarried.

Lady Mary Talbot

L ADY MARY TALBOT's marriage to William, 3rd Earl of
Pembroke, on November 4th 1604, was the occasion for a
great tournament at Wilton.[1] The bride's pedigree was impressive.
Her father was Gilbert Talbot, 7th Earl of Shrewsbury; her mother,
Mary Cavendish, was a daughter of the formidable Elizabeth
Cavendish, Bess of Hardwick. And her godmother was an even
more illustrious Mary, Mary Stuart, Queen of Scots. Amidst this
Marian deluge the reader will have noted that Mary Talbot's aunt,
Katherine Talbot, had been the second wife of the 2nd Earl, and
that all three of the Pembroke Earls to date had married a Talbot
at some time in their lives.

Mary Sidney approved of her son's match. Some of the
Talbots, however, had been wary of Pembroke. He was a known
womaniser; an affair with Mary Fitton, one of Queen Elizabeth's
maids of honour, had resulted in Mary Fitton falling pregnant.
Lord Herbert, as he then was, defied even the Queen in refusing
to marry her.[2] Why then should he want to marry Mary Talbot?
Some writers – though their view is subjective and unconfirmed
by contemporary portraits – maintain that Mary was 'dwarfish
and unattractive.' The reality is that we know very little about
her beyond that she was born c. 1580, contracted measles when a
girl, and became a Gentlewoman of the Privy Chamber to Queen
Elizabeth as a young woman.[3] What she incontrovertibly was,
however, was a wealthy heiress; hence the surmise that Pembroke

1   Lever, *Herberts of Wilton*, p. 70. William, son of the 2nd Earl and
Mary Sidney, became 3rd Earl of Pembroke in 1600.
2   Talbot Papers 3202, fol. 259, Mary Sidney to Shrewsbury, 29 Sept.
1604; Lever, *Herberts of Wilton*, pp. 61-62, 64-69.
3   Lever, *Herberts of Wilton*, p. 70; Talbot Papers 3202, fol. 398,
Elizabeth Wingfield to Lady Talbot nd (25 May 1580s).

7. *Lady Mary Talbot by Cornelius Johnson (Wikimedia Commons)*

married Mary chiefly for her inheritance. Edward Hyde, Earl of Clarendon, writing in the later 1640s, judged that Mary was 'a great addition' to the Herbert family but that Pembroke 'paid much too dear for his wife's fortune, by taking her person into the bargain'.[1]

1　Clarendon, *The History of the Rebellion and Civil Wars in England*, Oxford, new ed., 1807, I, pp. 88-89.

Clarendon was being unduly cynical. Pembroke had no desperate need for money and Mary Talbot did not inherit the third of her father's fortune which was her due until 1616. What Pembroke saw in 1604 was a vivacious young woman who would make a suitable wife. A few weeks after the wedding, Rowland Whyte, a family friend, was reporting of the marriage that 'My Lady much joys in it, and gives him [Pembroke] every day more cause to increase it'.[1] The few references to the new Countess which exist suggest that she was a young woman who continued to enjoy the masques and other entertainments which characterised the early Stuart Court. In October 1606, for example, Mary was present at a ball in Hampton Court following which Whyte observed that 'No lady there did dance near so well as she did that day.' The Countess played host to King James I and Queen Anne when they visited Wilton the same year.[2]

Such self-indulgence, it has to be admitted, does not make Mary Talbot a figure of much significance. She gave birth to only one child, a son named Henry, but he died in infancy. The Pembroke title would not descend by her, a factor perhaps which contributed to a decline in the happiness of her marriage.

Following the Earl's death in 1630, Mary lived at Baynard's Castle in London and Ramsbury Manor near Marlborough. As Dowager Countess of Pembroke she outlived her husband by nearly twenty years before being laid alongside him, in the Pembroke family vault in Salisbury Cathedral, following her death on January 25th 1650.[3]

---

1   Lever, *Herberts of Wilton*, p. 70.
2   M. Brennan, N. Kinnamon & M. Hannay (eds), *Letters of Rowland Whyte to Sir Robert Sidney*, pp. 566-7; Lever, *Herberts of Wilton*, pp. 76-77.
3   Lever, *Herberts of Wilton*, pp. 99, 115.

LADY SUSAN DE VERE

LADY SUSAN DE VERE was born on May 26th 1587. She was the youngest surviving daughter of Edward de Vere, 17th Earl of Oxford, a patron of the arts regarded by some Shakespeare doubters as at least part author of his plays. Her mother was Anne Cecil, daughter of William Cecil, Lord Burghley, the greatest servant of the Elizabethan state. It was in Burghley's household that the infant Susan went to live following her mother's death in 1588. It was also, by dint of Burghley's generosity, that Lady Susan became a wealthy woman: when he died in 1598 she inherited assets valued at £7,767 together with property yielding an annual rental of £230.[1] Still barely eleven, Susan was then assigned to the custody of her uncle, Robert Cecil (later Earl of Salisbury), who emerged as chief minister to King James I when he ascended the English throne in 1603. It was presumably Uncle Robert who, by 1604, had helped to secure her a position at Court as a Lady of the Drawing Chamber to the new Queen, Anne of Denmark.

Lady Susan had assured Robert Cecil in 1602 that she would 'never match with any without your consente'.[2] Two years later she broke her word when, on December 27th 1604, she married Philip Herbert, brother of the 3rd Earl, in secret. Pembroke relayed the news to a less than happy Cecil that 'after long love, & many changes, my brother on Fryday last was privately contracted to my La. Susan without the knowledg of any of his or her friends'.[3] Fortunately for her, Philip Herbert was a favourite with the royals. Henry, Prince of Wales, escorted Lady Susan to the royal chapel in Whitehall; King James I himself played the

---

1   *ODNB*, 'Susan de Vere'.
2   *ODNB*, 'Susan de Vere'.
3   Talbot Papers 3021, fol. 225.

role of father by giving her away, as well as presenting her with a wedding gift of land worth £500 on the Isle of Sheppey. It was, however, perhaps taking things a bit too far when he visited Susan and Philip the morning after their wedding night when he 'spent a good hower with them in the bed or uppon chuse wch you will believe best'. But indulging the royal intrusion paid dividends: Susan and Philip were created Countess and Earl of Montgomery on May 4th 1605.[1]

Both her new sister-in-law, Mary, Countess of Pembroke, and Susan, Countess of Montgomery, revelled in revels.[2] Susan is one of only two women whose names appear in all the Court masques to have been performed at Queen Anne's behest. These included Ben Jonson's *The Masque of Blackness* (1605), *Hymenaei* (1606), *The Masque of Beauty* (1608), and *The Masque of Queens* (1609). Unlike the Pembroke Countess, however, Countess Susan appears to have been held in much higher regard by the literary circles in which she moved. Jonson hailed her as 'a new Susanna, equal to that old.' The poet George Chapman addressed her as 'Great and Virtuous'; another writer, Augustine Taylor, lauded her 'pious bounties' and 'religious wisedome'. Doubtless this was part motivated by sycophancy and a desire to ingratiate themselves with her politically influential uncle (Cecil), husband (Montgomery), and friend (Queen Anne), but it was surely also because Susan was interested in what they did. In 1619 she asked John Donne to send her a copy of one of his recently delivered sermons. The same year, possibly because Susan had been able to raid Mary Sidney's library at Wilton, the playwright Anthony Munday acknowledged 'the help of that worthy Lady, I have had such Bookes as were of the best editions' for his translation of *Amadis de Gaule*. The latter was dedicated to her husband, but Susan too was the dedicatee of several works, most obviously Lady Mary Wroth's 1621 *The Countess of Montgomery's*

1   Lever, *Herberts of Wilton*, pp. 79-80; http://www.historyofparliamentonline.org/volume/1604-1629/member/herbert-sir-philip-1584-1650 accessed 17 Mar. 2022.
2   *ODNB*, 'Susan de Vere'.

Urania.[1]

Susan, Countess of Montgomery, was also amongst the most fecund of the Herbert wives. She is reckoned to have had seven sons and three daughters, though two sons and two daughters did not survive infancy.[2] Susan herself did not survive contracting smallpox; she died early in 1629 and was buried in the chapel of St Nicholas with other of her maternal relations in Westminster Abbey. Although Susan never lived long enough to become Countess of Pembroke (another year or so would have sufficed), her second son, Philip, lived to succeed as 5th Earl in 1649. In a sense, therefore, she was the mother of all subsequent Earls in that her title of Montgomery has descended, intertwined with that of Pembroke, to the present day.[3]

---

1   Mary Wroth (1587-c.1653) was Mary Sidney's niece.
2   Lever, *Herberts of Wilton*, p. 96n.
3   Her husband, Philip 1st Earl of Montgomery, became 4th Earl of Pembroke in 1630. The present 18th Earl of Pembroke is thus the 15th Earl of Montgomery.

LADY MARY VILLIERS AND A WILTON MYSTERY

VISITORS TO WILTON'S Great State Room, known popularly as the Double Cube Room, are irresistibly drawn to van Dyck's great family portrait. It depicts the 4th Earl and his family gathered to celebrate the marriage of his heir, Charles, Lord Herbert. The lady seated to the Earl's left was long identified as being Susan de Vere, wife and mother of the assembled company. The bulk of modern opinion inclines to doubt that it is her. Susan, Countess of Montgomery, it contends, was dead before van Dyck put brush to canvas. It is, therefore, the Earl's second wife, Lady Anne Clifford, dressed in black – her favourite colour – and appearing somewhat detached from events, at whom we are looking. The debate will doubtless continue.[1]

No doubt exists, however, that the star of the painting is Lady Mary Villiers. She was the daughter of George Villiers, 1st Duke of Buckingham, and Katherine Manners, Baroness de Ros. Left fatherless at the age of six in 1628 when her father, unpopular as royal favourite of Charles I, was assassinated, Lady Mary became a ward of the King. Her marriage had in fact already been agreed two years earlier when the 4th Earl struck a deal with Buckingham to unite her with his eldest surviving son, Charles. The wedding took place on January 8th 1635; Lady Mary's dowry was the stupendous sum of £25,000. But she would never be Countess of Pembroke. Charles died, aged sixteen, probably from smallpox, whilst travelling abroad in January 1636. The Earl had more sons

1   B. M. Cutting, 'A countess transformed: how Lady Susan Vere became Lady Anne Clifford,' *Brief Chronicles*, IV (2012–13), pp. 117–34; F. Russell, *Paintings and Drawings at Wilton House*, pp. 37-40. For what it is worth, the present authors are decidedly of the opinion that van Dyck's lady in black is a posthumous image of Susan de Vere.

8. Philip, 4th Earl of Pembroke, and his family by Sir Anthony van Dyck, c. 1635 [The Double Cube Room]

but he had to return the dowry.[1]

Lady Mary lived and prospered. She married James Stewart, 4th Earl of Lennox in 1637. The couple were further ennobled as Duke and Duchess of Richmond in 1641. Widowed for a second time in 1655, she took Colonel Thomas Howard, brother of Charles Howard, 1st Earl of Carlisle, as her third husband. She died in 1685. By then, as we shall see, Herbert family affairs had become much cause for gossip.

1   Lever, *Herberts of Wilton*, pp. 104-6.

LADY ANNE CLIFFORD

I T WAS TYPICAL of Anne Clifford's plain-speaking to say that she had been conceived on May 1st 1589. If she was right, she was born somewhat prematurely, at Skipton Castle in the West Riding of Yorkshire, on January 30th 1590. Anne was the only surviving child of George Clifford, 3rd Earl of Cumberland, and Lady Margaret Russell, daughter of the 2nd Earl of Bedford. The couple became estranged not long after Anne's birth; she was brought up chiefly in her mother's households in Buckinghamshire and Hertfordshire. These were almost exclusively female, the important exception being her tutor, Samuel Daniel. Poet, playwright and historian, Daniel had been part of Mary Sidney's circle at Wilton. He was an excellent teacher; Anne, an enthusiastic and able student. John Donne was to say that 'she knew well how to discourse of all things, from predestination to slea-silk'. She also benefited from specialist instruction on playing the lute and dance.[1]

As a young girl, Anne Clifford was said to have made a favourable impression upon the elderly Queen Elizabeth. As a teenager she put her education to good use in performances alongside Queen Anne of Denmark in Court masques. With the Queen reduced to the role of spectator, Anne is also known to have taken part in Ben Jonson's *The Masque of Beauty* (1608) and *The Masque of Queens* (1609). She would have been cognisant, therefore, of Susan de Vere, Countess of Montgomery, another who graced the floor on those occasions. She also knew Mary Talbot, Countess of Pembroke: in January 1617 the two were amongst a select party that ate 'a scrambling supper' at the Duke of Buckingham's lodgings.[2]

1   *ODNB*, 'Anne Clifford'.
2   D. Clifford (ed), *The Diaries of Lady Anne Clifford*, p. 44.

Although the adult Anne Clifford was diminutive – she was less than five feet tall – she was blessed with a comely figure, complemented by brown eyes and waist length brown hair. And since it was well known that she had inherited the enormous sum of £15,000 and the title of 14th Baroness de Clifford when her father died in 1605, she experienced no shortage of suitors. Having lobbied Anne's mother, the victors in the chase for 'that virtuous young lady' were the Sackvilles. A marriage agreement was concluded in 1607; the ceremony itself took place in 1609 when the nineteen year old Anne joined hands with Richard Sackville, 3rd Earl of Dorset. Their union was unhappy: he was a spendthrift womaniser; she displayed her lifelong tendencies to be both feisty and stubborn. Anne cannot have been unduly disconsolate when Sackville died in 1624. But she idolised the two daughters she had by him, and was as devoted to defending their interests as her mother had been to hers.[1]

Shortly after the Earl of Dorset's demise, Anne contracted smallpox, 'which disease did so martyr my face, that it confirmed more and more my mind never to marry again'. As her diary tells us however (she was unusual for the time in having kept one), 'the Providence of God caused me after to alter that resolution'.[2] Her necessary caveats were that her spouse be neither a courtier, nor encumbered by children or 'a great curser and swearer'. On June 3rd 1630 she duly ignored her own good advice – she well knew that he failed on all counts – when she married the widower Philip Herbert, 4th Earl of Pembroke.[3]

Why did Anne, a canny and experienced woman, do it? The suggestion that it was a response to having been discomfited by burglars in 1626 is unconvincing: four years is a long time to wait before summoning aid. Her own explanation (love it might be noted, is not mentioned) is more plausible: 'This 2nd marriage of myne was wonderfullie brought to pass by ye Providence of God for the Crossing and disappoynting, the envie, malice and

1   *ODNB*, 'Anne Clifford'.
2   Lever, *Herberts of Wilton*, pp. 98-99.
3   M. Holmes, *Proud Northern Lady*, p. 126.

9. Lady Anne Clifford, unknown artist, 1620, (Wikimedia Commons)

sinister practices of my Enemyes.'[1] Though Anne did not name them, those enemies are easy to identify. Her father had willed the bulk of his property to her uncle, Francis, who became 4th Earl of Cumberland in 1605. Anne and her mother believed this to be illegal; the latter, because Anne was only fifteen at the time, instituted proceedings for the restitution of acres she believed to be rightly her daughter's. The adult Anne carried on the fight, in which the Earl of Dorset assisted, but his death removed

1   Clifford, *Diaries of Lady Anne Clifford*, p. 91.

both financial and political supports from her which marrying the Earl of Pembroke would replace. She was right. Indeed, since the Herbert estates were wealthier than those of her late husband's, and Pembroke was a favourite of Charles I as his Lord Chamberlain, those supports would be strengthened.

For all that Anne's marriage was calculating, outwardly at least, it appears to have started well enough. Although neither survived infancy, she bore the Earl two sons. With his help, she was able to complete her mother's plan for alms houses near Skipton. Locally, she struck up a friendship with the newly appointed rector of Bemerton, George Herbert. One of the great poet's few surviving letters, dated December 10th 1631, thanks Anne for 'admitting our poor services', and also for the present of a cask of metheglin [spiced mead].[1] Above all, however, Anne and Philip were able to bask in the royal favour that derived from the fact that King Charles I 'first did love Wilton above all places, and came thither every summer'.[2] It must have been during the early years of their marriage that Charles put it to them that Wilton might be made more grandiose. The result was the creation of the Inigo Jones-inspired State Apartment for which the house is famous today.

Anne's biographers have been apt to trumpet her role in the first great refashioning of Wilton since the 1st Earl of Pembroke created the house nearly a century earlier. The standard history of the Herbert family, which describes Anne, far from accurately, as eccentric, impetuous and lavish in her tastes, accuses her of having egged her husband on.[3] There is certainly a prima facie case to be made. Anne was living at Wilton when the project was first mooted. She was interested in architecture: she had set up a memorial to Edmund Spenser in Westminster Abbey as early as 1620. Furthermore, Inigo Jones designed some of the dresses

1   A. James, *A Life of George Herbert*, pp. 171-3. We would like to thank Peter Webster and Lesley Burton for answering our queries concerning George Herbert.
2   Clark, *John Aubrey's Brief Lives*, I, p. 312.
3   Holmes, *Proud Northern Lady*, pp. 129-30.

which she wore at Court masques; and Isaac de Caux, who was to execute much of the work at Wilton, was also employed by Anne to create a gatehouse at Skipton Castle.[1] But the hard evidence is lacking. From a chronological point of view at least, the case for Anne's involvement is limited. She had left Wilton well before 1636 when work on the new south wing started, and was living back in the North by the time its tortuous gestation was complete. The Earl, with firm views about what he wanted, was clearly the driving force. It is, on balance, less likely that they cooperated on the venture than that they bickered over its details thereby adding to difficulties in a relationship that was rapidly turning sour.[2]

Frictions between Anne and Philip came to a head at the end of 1634. Anne's diary entry for December 18th records that 'by reason of some Discontent, I went from living at ye Court at Whitehall to live at Baynards Castle in London, where & at his [Pembroke's] houses in Wilton & Ramsbury I continued to live for ye most part during ye time of his life after'.[3] The nature of the 'discontent' is unspecified. Suggestions that have been proffered range from pre-Christmas tension(!) to Anne's dislike of the company Philip kept at Whitehall, and arguments about property. But perhaps it was just simply a question of two abrasive characters having the self-knowledge to accept that they would get along better by avoiding each other. This would certainly explain Pembroke's anger when Anne turned up, unannounced, at Whitehall, the 4th Earl's preferred abode when away from Wilton.[4]

The parting of the ways was not permanent: Anne sometimes appeared with the Earl on formal occasions. Philip was sufficiently well disposed towards her that, in June 1635, he made over to her a jointure in his lands in the Isle of Sheppey. He also relinquished

1   Holmes, *Proud Northern Lady*, p. 130; Robinson, *Wilton House*, p. 78.
2   Robinson, *Wilton House*, ch. 3, for the history of the new south wing.
3   Clifford, *The Diaries of Lady Anne Clifford*, p. 92.
4   Holmes, *Proud Northern Lady*, pp. 127-8.

any rights to her property in Westmorland, and assisted her when she pressed her formal claims to the Clifford estate in 1637.[1] When the English Civil War (the one between Crown and Parliament, not the Earl and Countess!) broke out in 1642, Anne acceded to Philip's request to live at Baynard's Castle in order to keep an eye on his possessions there.[2] Even so, there was another major falling out, perhaps more of a running sore bursting, when Anne refused to let Philip marry off one of his younger sons by Susan de Vere to Isabella, one of Anne's daughters by the Earl of Dorset. This was presumably what Anne was alluding to in her diary for May 1645 when she wrote that 'some yeares before' there had been 'a great cause of Anger & falling out between my Lord and mee.' Pembroke was furious when Isabella married James Compton, 3rd Earl of Northampton, in 1647.[3]

Anne saw Pembroke in Whitehall on June 3rd 1649, their nineteenth wedding anniversary. The Civil Wars were over and King Charles I was dead. More germane to her interests, the coming of peace allowed Anne to leave Baynard's Castle and depart for the North. She would do so in triumph: her cousin Henry had succeeded to the Clifford estates as 5th Earl of Cumberland in 1641 but had died without a male heir in 1643, meaning that Anne could at last take charge of her father's property. She reached Skipton Castle on July 18th, the first time that she had been there since she was born.[4] Less than six months later she would hear of her husband's passing. He was, she reflected, 'no scholler at all to speak of … Yet he was of a verie quick apprehension, a sharp understanding, verie craftie withal, and of a discerning spirit, but extremely chollerick by nature which was increased the more by the office of Lord Chamberlain to the King'. Less generous in his

1　Clifford, *The Diaries of Lady Anne Clifford*, p. 92.
2　During the war Anne was a Royalist, Philip a moderate Parliamentarian. It was typical of the couple to want to have a foot in both camps!
3　Clifford, *The Diaries of Lady Anne Clifford*, p. 96. Pembroke, of course, had an eye to the Clifford fortune which was by then likely to fall to Anne and her heirs.
4　Clifford, *The Diaries of Lady Anne Clifford*, p. 100.

will than she was in her assessment, Pembroke bequeathed her just £500.[1]

With Philip dead and her property secure, Anne lived to enjoy her Northern inheritance as a landowner, philanthropist and patron of the arts. She augmented her library, 'stored with very choice books, which she read over, not cursorily, but with judgement and observation'. She kept a particular lookout for antiquarian volumes which could buttress her claims to the family inheritance. Possibly inspired by the Wilton diptych, she commissioned a triptych to consummate those claims and her life history in art: although Pembroke appears in it, he does so with only the briefest of biographical details.[2] Anne also used her income of £8,000 per annum – she was 'perhaps the wealthiest noblewoman in later Stuart England' – to build a legacy brick by brick. She repaired family property damaged in the Great Rebellion, restored churches, and erected alms houses. There were also, revealingly, monuments to her mother, and her erstwhile tutor, Samuel Daniel.[3]

Anne died at Brougham Castle in Yorkshire on March 22nd 1676. She was buried in St Lawrence's Church, Appleby-in-Westmorland. Unsurprisingly, she designed the vault herself. She never saw Wilton before 1630 and never saw it again after October 12th 1642. Paradoxically, though she was Countess of Pembroke and Montgomery for nearly twenty years, and arguably Wilton's most formidable chatelaine, she never fell in love with the place. Its marbled pillars, she wrote, 'were to mee oftentimes but the gay Arbours of Anguish … I gave myself wholly to Retyredness as much as I could… and made good books and vertuous thoughts my companions.'[4] Her anguish, of course, arose in large part from her unhappy marriage but it was also something more. Anne

1   Lever, *Herberts of Wilton*, pp. 116-17.
2   Holmes, *Proud Northern Lady*, p. 140. The Wilton diptych, dating to the 1390s, and the pride of Wilton's art collection until it was sold to the National Gallery in 1929, may have been purchased by the 4th Earl.
3   *ODNB*, 'Anne Clifford'.
4   Clifford, *The Diaries of Lady Anne Clifford*, p. 94.

Clifford was, as her cousin Francis Russell, 4th Earl of Bedford, observed, like the River Rhone as it flowed through Geneva: a mighty river washing the banks as it rolled onwards but never quite losing its own identity.[1]

1   Holmes, *Proud Northern Lady*, pp. 128-9.

PENELOPE NAUNTON

PENELOPE NAUNTON, whose fine portrait by van Dyck sits in the Double Cube room at Wilton, married Philip, the 5th Earl in 1639. She was the daughter of Sir Robert Naunton, a writer and politician, and Penelope Perrot, granddaughter of Walter Devereux, 1st Earl of Essex. Her first husband, Paul, 2nd Viscount Bayning, of Honningham Hall in Norfolk, died in 1638. Penelope never became Countess of Pembroke, but she was the mother of William, who became the 6th Earl, the most colourless of their number, in 1669.

10. Penelope Naunton, engraving from a portrait by Sir Anthony van Dyck, c. 1640 (Wikimedia Commons)

CATHERINE VILLIERS

T WO YEARS AFTER Penelope died, the 5th Earl married
Catherine Villiers. Her father, Sir William Villiers, 1st

11. Catherine Villiers by Sir Peter Lely, c. 1660

Baronet Villiers of Brooksby in Leicestershire, was a half-brother of George Villiers, Duke of Buckingham, favourite of James I and Charles I, whose daughter Mary features in van Dyck's great family portrait of the Herberts. Unlike her distant cousin, however, Catherine did go on to be Countess of Pembroke, in 1619. She then became only the second (and final) Countess to give birth to two Lord Pembrokes, Philip, 7th Earl and Thomas, 8th Earl respectively. That said, the marriage was not entirely harmonious. In 1658 Catherine brought a petition to Parliament in which she accused her husband of unkindness, violence and cruelty. She also prayed for an order of maintenance – suggesting that they had already become estranged. Philip, 5th Earl, issued a counter-petition but the court found against him. Unsurprisingly, he left her little or nothing in his will. As Dowager Countess from 1669, she leased some land and hop gardens from her stepson, William, 6th Earl, but beyond that the record is silent.

Catherine, Countess of Pembroke, died in 1678, and so was spared the roller coaster story of Philip, her eldest son, who became 7th Earl in 1674. But she did live to see him married; it was a match to which she voiced vociferous opposition.[1]

1 Lever, *Herberts of Wilton*, p. 119.

HENRIETTE DE KÉROUAILLE

HENRIETTE MAURICETTE de Penancoët de Kérouaille was born in about 1651. Her parents, Guillaume de Penancoët, Count de Kérouaille, and Marie de Ploeuc de Timeur, hailed from Brittany. Henriette had a brother, Sebastien, but it was her elder sister, Louise, whose life history aroused the wrath of the Dowager Countess Catherine. As a teenager, Louise had entered the household of the Duchess of Orleans, better known in England as Henrietta Stuart, sister of Charles II. Henrietta introduced Louise, then 21, to the King, her brother, when Louise accompanied her on a visit to England in 1670. Henrietta's death only weeks later prompted Charles to appoint Louise as a maid of honour at the English Court. She soon graduated to become one of Charles' many (and soon chief) mistresses: he called her 'Fubbs' ('plump' or 'chubby', by no means a pejorative term at the time) and named the royal yacht after her. Nell Gwyn, a more celebrated mistress but less complimentary observer, took to calling her 'Squintabella'. Ms Gwyn, who did not like to be confused with her Catholic rival, was also at pains to point out to those that would damn her that 'I am the Protestant whore'. The Catholic one, Louise, bore Charles a son in 1672. Named Charles Lennox, he was created Duke of Richmond.[1] Louise was made Duchess of Portsmouth the following year. But it was neither Louise's rapid preferment, her religion, nor even her promiscuity which lay at the root of popular hostility towards her: the latter derived chiefly from her being French and the supposition (probably well grounded) that she was a spy in the service of Louis XIV.

1   The Dukes of Richmond at Goodwood House in West Sussex are descendants.

12. Henriette de Kérouaille by Sir Peter Lely, c. 1675

Henriette de Kérouaille, encouraged by her sister, came to England from Brest, apparently unchaperoned (in itself something a little scandalous), in May 1674. Henri de Massue, Earl of Galway – though beauty is in the eye of the beholder – reported that she was a young girl of no more than ordinary attraction. She was certainly sufficiently attractive to Charles II: doubtless at Louise's prompting, he granted Henriette a pension of £600 a year. This was not mere sisterly loyalty; the unpopular Louise sought to use Henriette as 'a means of securing herself English allies'. The ploy reaped almost immediate dividends since another who found Henriette more than ordinarily attractive was Philip Herbert. Newly succeeded as 7th Earl in July 1674, and popular at Court, he married her on December 17th 1674. A letter from the diplomat Simon Arnauld, Marquess de Pomponne, noted that Henriette 'was married on Thursday to the Earl of Pembroke, he being pretty well recovered from his pox. The King pays the wedding portion'. The 'wedding and the entertainment are to be on her Grace's account, at my Lady Shannon's house at Turnham Green' in Chiswick.[1]

Pomponne's letter refers, undiplomatically, to sexual issues but they did not prevent the couple from having a daughter: Lady Charlotte Herbert was born in 1676. This would prove the highpoint of the relationship. Henriette was living a separate life shortly thereafter. It was preferable to one with Pembroke, the nature of which is fearful even to imagine.[2] In November 1677 the Earl almost killed a man in a duel. Two months later his explosive temper caused him to utter what Lord Chancellor Finch described as 'such horrid and blasphemous words, and other actions proved upon oath, as are not fit to be repeated in any Christian assembly'. Pembroke was sent to the Tower but was released after just two days. Four days after that, on February 4th 1678, in what was probably a celebratory binge, he killed a man in a drunken scuffle in a Haymarket tavern. The following day he assaulted another man in The Strand, before standing trial for murder in April. Found guilty of the lesser charge of manslaughter, he claimed peer's privilege: his punishment consisted only in having to pay his legal fees. Having reached what most people might consider to be rock bottom, Pembroke managed to drill deeper when, following another drunken carousal in August 1680, he killed an officer of the watch at Turnham Green. Convicted of murder in June 1681, he escaped the axe by virtue of a royal pardon, the granting of which owed something, one suspects, to the pillow

1   H. Forneron, *Louise de Keroualle*, pp. 110-11.
2   *ODNB*, 'Philip, 7th Earl of Pembroke'.

talk of Henriette's sister. But at least the Earl liked animals. He was banished to Wilton where, as John Aubrey records, he resided with '52 mastives and 30 grey-hounds, some beares, and a lyon, and a matter of 60 fellowes more bestial then they'. He died in August 1683, aged 30, and is buried, perhaps not altogether deservedly, in Salisbury Cathedral.[1]

We do not know what Henriette made of her husband's descent into depravity. She left Wilton, and probably England, soon after 1676. In 1682 she was certainly back in her native France and living in Paris. Records survive suggesting that she found some solace in retail therapy: that year she bought '28 pairs of open work white gloves, with orange and amber scent and one pair of gloves costing 33 livres, trimmed with ribbon, gold and silver on the arms, and herringboned in gold and silver on the back of the hand'.[2] There is a story that she, still Countess after all, returned to England to visit the 7th Earl at Wilton, aspiring perhaps, however quixotically, to 'rescue' him. But this feels improbable and in any event she did not stay long.

It was Pembroke's death in 1683 that galvanised Henriette into action. The new Dowager Countess chartered several ships and ransacked Wilton House, as well as the family's London property, in search of pretty much anything that could be carried off back to France. One colourful account has her sewing jewels into the hems of her dresses but it would have needed the ships, not the dresses, to transport her cargo of booty. It included chests full of silk moire, Indian textiles richly embroidered with silver thread, Welsh flannel, 204 pairs of gloves (a particular fetish it would appear, given the twenty nine pairs she bought in Paris in 1682!), and thirteen pairs of silk stockings. Amongst items of furniture she took, the most eye-catching was a bed with its hangings of brocade and crimson Genoa velvet, but also cabinets (notably a grand cabinet of old Chinese lacquer), other Chinese style furniture, chaises, sedan chairs, gueridons (round tables),

---

1   Clark, *John Aubrey's Brief Lives*, I, p. 317; *ODNB*, 'Philip, 7th Earl of Pembroke'.
2   Forneron, *Louise de Keroualle*, pp. 110-11.

mirror frames and tapestries. Further miscellaneous items removed from the house included 30 lbs of mocha coffee, four bales of soap, a chest of chocolate, a chest of Greek currants, spices, 100lbs of best wax tapers, 100lbs of pins and needles, and much expensive jewellery.[1]

With Pembroke's financial affairs in the most predictable of messes, Henriette also began litigation against the Wilton estate. This was done partly with a view to securing what she believed was hers according to her marriage jointure, but also to ensure that her daughter, Charlotte, received her marriage portion of £10,000. In these endeavours she encountered stiff opposition from her brother-in-law, Thomas Herbert, now 8th Earl. The latter, to be fair, had an estate to salvage and a brother's debts to pay. But he also enjoyed the advantage of knowing more about English law. We may infer as much from a letter Henriette wrote to the lawyer, John Romsey, in 1687. She 'did much importune' him to 'assist her in the management' of her estate and to 'advise and direct her how to proceed therein, as she is not knowing how to comply with what was required of her'. As they grew up, both Henriette's daughter, and then granddaughter, took up the cudgels in an attempt to secure what they believed was their legal entitlement. In June 1724 the septuagenarian 'H. Pembroke' wrote imploring her great nephew, Charles, 2nd Duke of Richmond, to 'avoir la charité pour un pauvre vieille tante'.[2] By then the Herbert land in South Wales, which she had hoped would be hers, had been mostly swallowed up by the lawyers in legal fees.[3]

Henriette's personal life, by contrast, had a comparatively happy epilogue. Having retired briefly to a French convent, she re-emerged in 1685 to marry Timoleon Gouffier, Marquess de Thois. She bore him nine children, at least four of whom reached adulthood. Charlotte, her daughter by the 7th Earl, married

1   Forneron, *Louise de Keroualle*, esp. chs 5, 11, 12.
2   Goodwood Papers 112, Henriette de Kérouaille to Richmond, 28 June 1724.
3   For examples of the litigation see National Archives, C8/514/49; C8/563/18; C8/274/26; C8/640/53-56.

John Jeffreys, soon to be 2nd Baron Jeffreys, son of the notorious 'Hanging Judge', George Jeffreys, in 1688. The marriage was an unhappy one (John Jeffreys was a drunkard) but their union produced a daughter, Henrietta Louisa (1698-1761). Although her grandmother did not live to see it, Henrietta Louisa became Countess of Pomfret and, as Henrietta Fermor, an English letter writer of some distinction.[1] Charlotte, who became Baroness Jeffreys in 1689, was widowed in 1702. Her second marriage, in 1703, to Thomas, 1st Viscount Windsor, proved far happier. Mindful of her ancestry, their first son was named Herbert. Viscountess Charlotte died in 1733.

As for Henriette, she died at her home in the Rue de Varennes in Paris on May 12th 1725. She was buried in the grand church of Saint-Sulpice. Her death certificate states, with charming Gallic phonetics and disregard for detail, that she was the widow of 'Thomas Arbock Earl of Pimbrooch'.[2]

1   *ODNB,* 'Henrietta Fermor'.
2   Forneron, *Louise de Keroualle,* p. 306. It should of course read 'Philip Herbert, Earl of Pembroke'.

MARGARET SAWYER

THOMAS HERBERT, 8th Earl of Pembroke from 1683, is invariably lauded as the man who not only saved but greatly enhanced Wilton and its treasures. His catalogue of achievements is impressive. Active in public life as a soldier, administrator and diplomat, he rose to become Lord High Admiral in 1702. Three years earlier, he had laid the foundations for the carpet making business in Wilton that would win international renown. He earned his sobriquet of 'the collector Earl' by amassing a collection of coins, Old Masters, and antique statuary of near peerless size and quality. Likeable and eccentric (Queen Mary II pithily described him 'as mad as most of his family, tho' very good natured'), Pembroke was a close friend of the philosopher John Locke, ribbed by the poet Alexander Pope, and rubbed shoulders with the likes of Sir Isaac Newton.[1] And although Earl Thomas was often duped and overly imaginative (some paintings were by inferior hands; many busts 'stubbornly "rebaptised" with names of his own choosing'), it remains true that Wilton's collections are amongst the finest to be seen in any English stately home.[2]

An obvious question nevertheless remains: from where did the 8th Earl obtain the funds to indulge his passion? His profligate and murderous brother, Philip, had left Wilton in a parlous state of debt, yet from the 1710s onwards, Earl Thomas thought nothing of lavishing £200 on a single antique bust. Part of the answer to this financial conundrum, as has not fully been appreciated, lies in his having contracted three advantageous marriages.

Margaret Sawyer became the Earl's first wife (and thus immediately Countess) when they married on July 26th 1684.

1   P. Stewart, *A Catalogue of the Sculpture Collection at Wilton House*, pp. 27, 31.
2   Stewart, *Catalogue of the Sculpture Collection*, pp. 6-11.

13. Margaret Sawyer by Jan van der Vaart, 1687

She was the only daughter of 'the wealthy and eminent lawyer', Sir Robert Sawyer (1633-1692). Sir Robert, of Highclere House in Hampshire, was a former Speaker of the House of Commons, and Attorney General at the time of his daughter's nuptials. For all his eminence, however, there was no mistaking that Margaret's marriage represented a considerable step up the social ladder for the Sawyers. By the same token, it should be noted, no previous Earl of Pembroke had married a woman of such common origins.

But Margaret seems to have coped admirably: when she was first presented at Court to Charles II's Queen, Catherine of Braganza, in September 1684, she conducted herself 'with competent assurance'.[1]

It is not known exactly how much Margaret brought to the Herbert family coffers. However, it does seem reasonable to conclude, taken in conjunction with a large dispersal sale of Wilton effects in 1685, and the Earl's pensions as a public servant, that the estate was secure by the time Margaret died at Werrington, aged 49, after 22 years as Countess, on November 27th 1706. Even more secure, it must be noted, was the Herbert succession. Margaret had given birth to seven sons and five daughters, comfortably (perhaps uncomfortably) the highest number of children hatched by any Countess. Branches of the Herbert tree might, and have, fallen off since, but thanks to Margaret it would require a genealogical disaster of near apocalyptic proportions to fell the tree itself.

Sir Robert Sawyer had left Highclere to his wife in 1692 with the provision that it should pass to Margaret and her younger sons thereafter. Since Margaret predeceased her mother by two years, Highclere passed to Margaret's second son, Robert Herbert, in 1708. When he died without surviving male issue in 1769, Highclere passed to his nephew (Margaret's grandson via her fifth son, William) Henry Herbert (1741-1811). Henry prospered to become 1st Earl of Carnarvon of the third creation in 1793. During the 1840s, Henry's grandson, the 3rd Earl of Carnarvon, employed Sir Charles Barry to build the grand new home known today as Highclere Castle, immortalised in the early twenty first century as Downton Abbey. The 5th Earl financed the archaeological excavations which culminated with the discovery of the tomb of Tutankhamun in 1922. Margaret Sawyer's legacy has therefore been an impactful one. And were the senior Herbert male line at Wilton to fail, an intermittent possibility over the past two centuries, the Herberts at Highclere would inherit the Wilton estate.[2]

1   Lever, *Herberts of Wilton*, p. 143.
2   *ODNB*, 'Thomas, 8th Earl of Pembroke'.

Barbara Slinsgby

Barbara Slinsgby became the 8th Earl's second Countess when they married on September 21st 1708. Barbara was the daughter of a Yorkshire baronet, Sir Thomas Slingsby, and the heiress Dorothy Cradock. This was in fact her third marriage:

14. Barbara Slingsby by Michael Dahl, c. 1708

she had outlived Sir Richard Mauleverer, and John, 2nd Baron Arundell. The Countess bore Pembroke two daughters before she died on August 1st 1721.[1]

1   *ODNB*, 'Thomas, 8th Earl of Pembroke'.

The Honourable Mary Howe

F OUR YEARS LATER, on June 24th 1725, the Honourable
Mary Howe succeeded Barbara as Countess of Pembroke.
She was the daughter of Scrope, 1st Viscount Howe, courtier and
MP, and the Honourable Juliana Alington, daughter of William,
3rd Baron Alington. The marriage of the popular 69 year old Earl
(by now generally known as 'Old Pem'), to a lady in her early
twenties was the source of 'much pleasantry at court'.[1] But Mary,
the new Countess of Pembroke, also proved popular. Already
a maid of honour to Caroline of Ansbach, Princess of Wales,
Mary became a Lady of the Bedchamber when Caroline became
George II's Queen in 1727. In October 1727 Mary was entrusted
with carrying the train of Queen Caroline at the coronation
in Westminster Abbey. The 8th Earl, who died in 1733, left
her £2,000 in his will. The Dowager Countess remarried John
Mordaunt MP; she died in 1749.[2]

1   ODNB, 'Thomas, 8th Earl of Pembroke'. Mary Howe's date of birth
is unknown but since her elder brother was born in 1700, a date of
1702/3 does not seem unreasonable.
2   ODNB, 'Thomas, 8th Earl of Pembroke'.

THE HONOURABLE MARY FITZWILLIAM

I T WAS THE Honourable Mary Fitzwilliam, born in 1707, another maid of honour to Caroline, Princess of Wales, and not much younger than Mary Howe, who was destined to become the next Countess of Pembroke. But Mary was joining hands with Henry the 9th Earl, not Thomas the 8th Earl, when she married Henry Herbert in August 1733. They presumably met at Court for Henry, Lord Herbert (he became 9th Earl on January 22nd 1733), was a Gentleman of the Bedchamber to George II.

The new Countess was daughter of the Irish peer, Richard, 5th Viscount Fitzwilliam, and Frances Shelley. Both were Roman Catholics but Mary and her siblings were baptised into the Church of England. Her name had been linked with a number of suitors, including (in 1728) Henry Grey, Duke of Kent, before she transferred her affections to Henry, 9th Earl of Pembroke.[1] Although the latter is known to have had mistresses, the marriage appears to have been a happy one. Henry, who became a Privy Councillor in 1734 and Groom of the Stool in 1735, referred to Mary affectionately as 'Rib'.[2] He was even more eccentric than his father, at least if one deems snacking on raw spinach and beetroot kept in a decorative bag tied to the back of his wig as eccentric. Henry was also hot-tempered – woe betides anybody who bested him at tennis. All in all we might presume that Mary was either a long suffering or an emollient wife.[3]

Mary, 'a great architect herself', according to the Duchess of Marlborough, appreciated her husband's talent for design: when good tempered, his achievements included the first Westminster

1   J.W. Croker (ed), *Letters to and from Henrietta, Countess of Suffolk*, I, p. 307.
2   J. Lees-Milne, *Earls of Creation*, p. 66.
3   *ODNB*, 'Henry Herbert, 9th Earl of Pembroke'.

*15. The Honourable Mary Fitzwilliam and Cupid by William Hoare,
c. 1740*

Bridge and the Palladian Bridge in Wilton Park.[1] The couple also shared a love of classical antiquity and archaeology and were, what we might now call, forward thinking (alternatively foolish). In 1739, for example, they exposed their only son and heir, five year old Henry, to variolation, a form of immunisation by which the young Lord Herbert was deliberately infected with a small amount of the smallpox virus.

Mary was widowed in 1750; she remarried in 1751. Her new husband was Major North Ludlow Barnard (1705-1768),

1   Lees-Milne, *Earls of Creation*, p. 67.

an army officer and a commoner. As such the match was much
frowned upon in high circles. Mary's attempt to improve matters
by instructing her spouse to sell his commission succeeded only in
adding ridicule to the situation. That great man of letters, Horace
Walpole, wrote in October 1751 that 'she was a favourite [at
Court] but has disgraced herself by marrying Captain Barnard'.
At least Walpole was being discreet. George II said within earshot
of Mary that 'I can't bear when women of quality marry one don't
know whom!'[1] But the marriage was happy and lasted seventeen
years until Barnard died in 1768.

Mary herself died in 1769, probably from jaundice, at the
Herberts' then London home, Pembroke House, in Whitehall.
She was buried in St Mary's, Wilton, with her first husband,
the 9th Earl. Mary had lived to see her son, Henry, 10th Earl,
married in 1759 and the birth of a grandson, George Augustus,
in 1759 but she was, as we shall see, distressed by the former's
errant behaviour thereafter.[2] Her greatest contribution to the
Pembroke family, and it was considerable, was in death, and came
about nearly half a century later. Her marriage had brought the
Herberts and Fitzwilliams closely together: her son, Henry, 10th
Earl, and Richard, 7th Viscount Fitzwilliam, her nephew, were
friends and cousins. The latter was, to all intents and purposes,
appointed MP for Wilton by the Herberts in 1790. Despite a
well-publicised affair with a French dancer, by whom he had three
children, Fitzwilliam died unmarried in 1816. The Fitzwilliam
title passed to his brother but the Fitzwilliam estate, which was
largely his to dispose of, was bequeathed to George Augustus,
by now 11th Earl of Pembroke, Mary's grandson.[3] Pembroke
family lore has it that Viscount Fitzwilliam's decision was made

1   W.S. Lewis (ed), *The Yale Edition of Horace Walpole's Correspondence*,
XX, pp. 280-1.
2   C. Hicks, *Improper Pursuits*, pp. 119-22.
3   The Fitzwilliam title became extinct on the death of the 9th Viscount
in 1833. Other money and effects bequeathed by the 7th Viscount went
to the University of Cambridge and formed the basis for the Fitzwilliam
Museum which opened in 1848.

on a whim 'when one morning, at breakfast, the expectant heir [Lord Onslow, another relation] after helping himself to cream, brought the rim of his cup in contact with the rim of the cream jug, to prevent a drop from falling. Lord Fitzwilliam contended that this was ill-bred, and showed want of refinement, inasmuch Lord Onslow's lip might have touched the part of the cup which touched the rim of the jug […] his name was forthwith erased from the will'. It is a good story – what purports to be some of the offending crockery can be seen at Wilton to this day – but improbable. It was the family link with the Herberts established by Mary Fitzwilliam which provided the conduit, or at least the foundation, through which Fitzwilliam wealth passed to the Herberts of Wilton. In terms of acreage (2,301 acres in 1883) it was not an especially large estate. But centred on Mount Merrion overlooking Dublin Bay, they included the most desirable property in and around southern Dublin. The annual rental, at current monetary values, was in excess of £2,000,000. Nearly 400 miles away across the Irish Sea, those whose vision did not extend that far from Wilton never appreciated just how vital this wealth was to the maintenance of the Herbert family's English estate over the next century and more.[1]

1   R.E. Foster, *Sidney Herbert*, pp. 24-25.

LADY ELIZABETH SPENCER

L ADY ELIZABETH SPENCER and Henry Herbert, the only son of the 9th Earl and Mary Fitzwilliam, were a golden couple in the 1750s in much the same way that Anne Parr and Sir William Herbert had been during the 1530s. Alas, their story did not play out so happily, certainly not for Lady Elizabeth. There were also, because of Henry's various failings, deleterious consequences for the Wilton estate.

Born in 1737, Lady Elizabeth – also known as Betty – was the second daughter of Charles Spencer, 3rd Duke of Marlborough, and Lady Elizabeth Trevor. She boasted an illustrious pedigree: her Spencer forebears had been prominent since the fifteenth century; her great-grandparents were the military genius John Churchill, 1st Duke of Marlborough, and his formidable Duchess, Sarah Jennings.[1]

Betty and her siblings, Diana, George, and Charles, enjoyed a happy upbringing, spent principally at Langley Park in Buckinghamshire. Betty was especially close to her elder sister, but her brothers did not stint in their affection. They wrote regularly to her from Eton where they were in the same House as their new friend Henry, Lord Herbert. One can reasonably presume that it was through them that Henry became aware of Betty's existence. But Henry, born in 1734, had to leave school abruptly when he succeeded to the Pembroke title, aged just fifteen, in 1750. It is not known whether the Spencer brothers engineered any meetings between Henry and their sister. Following a brief engagement, however, on March 13th 1756, and to the joy of both families at what was evidently a love match, the twenty one

1   The Marlboroughs' daughter Anne (the Duke had no son who outlived him) had married Charles Spencer in 1700. As Sir Winston Churchill often reminded people, he was a Spencer Churchill.

year old Earl made the nineteen year old Betty his Countess.[1]

Despite Lady Pembroke having suffered a miscarriage in 1758, the marriage began well; an heir, George Augustus, was born on September 10th 1759. The Earl, meanwhile, prospered in his public life. He was appointed a Lord of the Bedchamber to the Prince of Wales in November 1756, a position he continued to occupy when the Prince became George III in 1760. In 1758 he became aide-de-camp to George II, a Lieutenant-Colonel in the 15th Light Dragoons in 1759, and a Major-General in 1761. The same year, as proof of his admission to being 'horse mad', the 10th Earl published *A Method of Breaking Horses, and Teaching Soldiers to Ride,* which would run into several editions.[2] For her part, Elizabeth, judged by Horace Walpole to be 'one of the most beautiful creatures in England', with 'the face of a Madonna', could not but be popular in society. She was a good horsewoman, enjoyed walking and rowing, and founded a Ladies' Club for a group of like-minded women. At the coronation of George III in September 1761 she headed the line of countesses, 'the picture of majestic modesty'.[3] What could possibly go wrong? The answer, sadly, was plenty.

Pembroke, the handsome cavalry officer, possessed of what Walpole called 'an assemblage of good fortune', but often called away by his military responsibilities, seems simply to have tired of the modest and perhaps too saccharine Elizabeth.[4] In 1762 he began an affair with Miss Catherine (Kitty) Hunter, the daughter of a fairly nondescript Member of Parliament. Kitty was admittedly pretty, 'but silly and in no degree as lovely as his own wife'. That infatuation had got the better of the Earl's judgement was confirmed when he peremptorily resigned his commissions,

1 Lord Herbert (ed), *The Pembroke Papers,* I, pp. 22-27; *ODNB,* 'Elizabeth Spencer'.
2 Herbert, *The Pembroke Papers,* I, pp. 29-30; *ODNB,* 'Henry Herbert, 10th Earl of Pembroke'.
3 Herbert, *The Pembroke Papers,* I, p. 31; Lever, *Herberts of Wilton,* p. 168.
4 Herbert, *The Pembroke Papers,* I, pp. 30-33; Lever, *Herberts of Wilton,* pp. 169-71.

16. Lady Elizabeth Spencer, mezzotint by Charles Turner after Sir George Hayter, 1824 (Wikimedia Commons)

dressed himself incognito as a sailor, and took ship with his paramour for the Continent. In face of the scandal, Betty was praised for her 'serenity and dignified conduct'. Lady Caroline Fox observed that 'young Lady P [was] very unhappy, but bears it better than expected'. The Earl's mother, the Dowager Countess (Mary Fitzwilliam), 'miserable to the last degree', also took the part of her daughter-in-law. Bizarrely, so in a way did Pembroke himself: he supposedly wrote a letter 'to witness to the virtue of Lady Pembroke, whom he says he has long tried in vain to make hate and dislike him'. Even more bizarrely, he suggested that Betty come and make up a *ménage à trois* at Utrecht. Betty did not entirely discount the idea, but her family did, and anyway the projected three became four when Kitty gave birth to a son in November.

Betty was, however, prepared to be reconciled with her errant husband when he returned to England in March 1763. The evidence is that she still loved him; and the fact of an eighteenth century nobleman fathering an illegitimate son was hardly unprecedented. What was fairly unusual, though, is that Betty was prepared to accept the child as one of the family at Wilton. But there were limits. The boy had been named Augustus Retnuh Reebkomp, a not very subtle anagrammatic attempt to disguise his Hunter-Pembroke parentage. Despite the Earl's wanting to change it to Herbert, the Countess was adamantine in her refusal to allow Augustus to be 'Herberted and unReebkompfed'.[1] Thanks largely to her broadmindedness, however, the Reebkomp episode can be said to have had a happy ending. Augustus grew up alongside his half-brother, George Augustus, Lord Herbert; the two became close. Granted the compromise surname of Montgomery, Augustus became a naval officer and was a Captain when he died in port, at Plymouth, in 1797. Of Betty, Major John Floyd, a family friend, judged that Augustus was 'as much indebted to her as it is possible for any human being to be to another'.[2] So indeed were his two children, in whose upbringing the then Dowager Countess Betty would play a part. His son, George Augustus Montgomery became, with Pembroke patronage, rector of Bishopstone. In due course the two were sufficiently respectful of each other that Betty nominated the Reverend George to act as one of her executors.[3]

Earl Henry, however, unable to change his spots, was soon to abuse Betty's forbearance towards him. During a trip to the continent in 1768 he fathered an illegitimate daughter. She was

---

1   Lever, *Herberts of Wilton*, p. 178.
2   Herbert, *The Pembroke Papers*, II, p. 38; S. Thomas, 'Captain Augustus Montgomery, RN (1762-1797): Wiltshire's forgotten aristocratic bastard', *Wiltshire Archaeological and Natural History Magazine*, CI (2008), pp. 213 25.
3   S. Thomas, 'Care in the Community: an example from 19th-century Wiltshire', *Wiltshire Archaeological and Natural History Magazine*, CII (2009), p. 302.

named Caroline Medkaff, her surname an anglicised version of Mebkoper – another anagram of Pembroke! To his credit, Henry provided for Caroline's education and was concerned to see her happily married. But when the latter event was in the offing in 1786 it was clear that he had never been brave enough to tell the Countess about his indiscretion. So, in an act of cowardice, he put his sons George and Augustus under pressure to break the ill tidings, offering only a lame 'I thought Ly Pemb might, somehow or other, have heard of her' in his defence.[1]

Despite their having had a daughter together in 1773 – she was, in deference to the Queen, christened Charlotte – physical relations between the Pembrokes ended soon after. When he deigned to be at Wilton the Earl's mood was frequently volatile; he brooked little argument and Betty was deeply unhappy. I am 'sadly vex'd & plagued lately', she wrote in 1779, 'which has made me cruelly nervous, if I can but get *free* with Charlotte for a couple of months this summer, it may set me up again'.[2] It helped a little that she had rooms on the first floor whilst Henry kept to the rooms he had created (known today as the Smoking Rooms) on the ground floor.

What did not help was Henry's continued financial profligacy. Foreign travel, high living, his passions for horses and dogs, the maintenance of mistresses and illegitimate children collectively threatened the good work his grandfather, Thomas, 8th Earl, had done in resurrecting the fortunes of the Wilton estate. By 1787 he reckoned that £30,000 was needed to cover his mounting debts.[3] In the interim he had resorted to selling Wilton treasures which, legally, were not his to dispose of. Rumour had it that Betty stashed some family jewels and heirlooms in the bank to safeguard them for the family. Two generations later, Henry's grandson, Sidney Herbert, referred ironically to 'the knavery of my worthy grandfather'. He suspected the family's First Folio of

1   Herbert, *The Pembroke Papers*, I, p. 41; Lever, *Herberts of Wilton*, pp. 174, 189-90.
2   Herbert, *The Pembroke Papers*, I, p. 194.
3   Herbert, *The Pembroke Papers*, II, p. 341

the works of William Shakespeare had been amongst the treasures sold to finance his lifestyle.[1] Grandmother Betty, meanwhile, had had to endure relatively straitened finances. She regularly had to use her 'pin money' to support her son or servants, and she could not always attend Court because she could not afford the necessary gowns. Her young daughter, Charlotte, was told that trips to Brighton would have to be curtailed because 'the state of our finances are such that there is doubts of my getting money to leave Town'. The ever unreasonable Henry refused to pay for her to visit their son, George Augustus, in Europe during his Grand Tour.[2]

The latter spat was indicative of Betty's concern for her son and Wilton's heir. Well-read herself, she supervised his education before he went to Harrow, and later selected trusted companions (and offered educational advice) for his Grand Tour. She adored George: in a letter to the tutor accompanying him on the Grand Tour she confessed that 'you do not know what a foolish thing a mother is; while I am writing about him, my eyes fill, so that I cannot see'.[3] And when George entered Parliament for the family seat in Wilton in 1780 she offered the sagacious advice – which he took – that he should do well to avoid the damaging factional squabbles of the time.[4] Something of his mother's tenacity, commonsense and rectitude, all of which George would need when rejuvenating the Wilton estate, after he became Earl, appears to have rubbed off on him.

As George reached adulthood (he turned 21 in 1780), Betty's attentions focused ever more on Charlotte, her six year old daughter. Of a trip to Brighton which the two had taken together in September 1779, she wrote that 'much did I & Charlotte want the Sea, I for old nerves, & she from having been let alone too long … and looks & is wonderfully better within these two days'.[5]

1   Foster, *Sidney Herbert*, pp. 16-17.
2   Herbert, *The Pembroke Papers*, I, pp. 78, 213, 216.
3   Herbert, *The Pembroke Papers*, I, p. 61.
4   http://www.historyofparliamentonline.org/volume/1754-1790/member/herbert-george-augustus-1759-1827 accessed 8 Mar. 2022.
5   Herbert *The Pembroke Papers*, I, pp. 259-60.

Charlotte, it seems, rarely enjoyed rude health. When she became dangerously ill in 1783 even Earl Henry was persuaded to join the family in search of a cure. Doctors advised going to Lausanne in Switzerland, but Charlotte died, most likely from tuberculosis, at Aix-en-Provence, on April 21st 1784. Lord Pembroke departed, leaving a grieving mother and his sons to oversee the return of Charlotte's body for burial in Wilton.[1]

Lady Pembroke's anxieties for her children's wellbeing were compounded by those for her sister, known popularly in society as Lady Di.[2] The unravelling of the latter's personal life made Betty's marital travails seem almost trivial by comparison. Born in 1734, Lady Di had married the womanising drunk Frederick St John, 2nd Viscount Bolingbroke, of Lydiard Park in Wiltshire.[3] In the eighteenth century world of aristocratic double standards, however, it was Lady Diana Spencer who faced social ostracism when Bolingbroke divorced her on grounds of adultery in 1768. Lady Di had indeed sought sanctuary for her unhappiness through an affair with Topham Beauclerk. Once freed to do so, she married him, but the marriage was far from perfect: Topham suffered from an addiction to laudanum and an aversion to soap. Betty wrote with feeling to her son in July 1779 that 'I have been almost distracted these ten days with miseries of my poor Sister's ... Husbands are dreadfull and powerfull Animals'.[4] Lady Di nevertheless bore Beauclerk three children before his death in 1780. One of them, Betty's niece Elizabeth, would have her own part to play in the Pembroke story.

Betty's own marriage limped along during the 1780s. Although Charlotte's death had thrown them together in 1784, the Earl had then meandered expensively through Europe until

1   Herbert *The Pembroke Papers*, II, pp. 256-8; Lever, *Herberts of Wilton*, pp. 187-8.
2   Diana, Princess of Wales (1961-1997), was a daughter of Edward, 8th Earl Spencer. The Spencer earldom dates to 1765. John, 1st Earl, was a cousin of the Lady Elizabeth and Lady Diana in the present study.
3   Hicks, *Improper Pursuits, passim*; F. Bevan, *The Ladies of Lydiard*, pp. 119-26.
4   Herbert, *The Pembroke Papers*, I, p. 208.

1787. He even had the temerity in October that year to ask George (direct correspondence between the two having more or less ceased): 'Have ye spoke to Ly P about her part (cutbacks)? She has, I should think, one maid, one man, & a groom more than is necessary, & perhaps you may find more useless expences chez elle'.[1] What was perhaps the final straw came after Pembroke returned to Wilton in 1788 and decorated his drawing room with prints of his new mistress Giovanna Zanerini, an Italian dancer well known in Paris as 'La Baccelli'. George protested at his father's gross insensitivity: 'Those prints have a little more meaning in them, when hanging up at Wilton, than being merely portraits of a professional person; they are, as you must very well know, the portraits of an object that brought matters to an issue which forced Lady P: to take the steps she did'.[2] The steps alluded to were Betty's removing both her possessions and herself, first to her brother's house in Berkeley Square, and then to what became her main home, Pembroke Lodge in Richmond Park. Yet even now the Earl had the effrontery to complain that it was a porter who had told him of her 'separating intentions … I ought to have been the first informed'.[3]

Pembroke Lodge, originally a mole catcher's cottage, but since much improved, had been a gift to Betty from the King. Even more than those with her immediate family, it was Betty's friendship with George III and Queen Charlotte that is best remembered now. It would prove to be something of a mixed blessing: the best proof of the royal favour (and also that the Earl had been temporarily forgiven) was the two night visit paid by the royal couple to Wilton in October 1778. Presumably putting on a united front, 'Lord and Lady Pembroke received their Royal guests and entertained them with great elegance, splendour, and becoming munificence'.[4] In 1779 an excited Lady Pembroke,

1   Herbert, *The Pembroke Papers*, II, p. 361.
2   Herbert, *The Pembroke Papers*, II, p. 382.
3   Herbert, *The Pembroke Papers*, II, p. 385.
4   Herbert, *Pembroke Papers*, I, pp. 138-40; *Hampshire Chronicle*, 5 Oct. 1778.

then staying at Windsor, wrote to her son that 'I have seen a great deal of the Royal Family here ... they have all been wonderfully civil to me & to [her daughter] Charlotte'.[1] She received official approbation when she was appointed a Lady of the Bedchamber in 1782 and it was as mother to mother that the Queen wrote to Betty following her daughter Charlotte's death in July 1784: 'I hope I need not add that I have & do now very strongly feel for your loss ... & I am pretty sure that though my dear Lady Pembroke's life has not hitherto proved to be very happy, that there will come a time that you will be rewarded for your sufferings ... Oh! may you both *be* & *feel* happy is my sincere wish'.[2]

The King's feelings for Betty, however, were born more of infatuation. They dated, so he claimed, to the early 1750s when they were both teenagers and she was still plain Betty Spencer. Based actually, one presumes, on his 'madness' and the fact that Betty was in close proximity to him at Court after 1782 the situation was, to say the least, embarrassing. Referring to her variously as Esther, Elizabeth and Minerva, the King's more lascivious letters made 'her handsome offers if she would be his mistress', 'with so much ardour and such splendid offers', judged one minister, 'that I tremble for her virtue'.[3] Even worse, however, were the letters written with the conviction that Betty was his Queen. He woke one morning to tell the Duke of Sussex: 'Is it not a strange thing, Adolphus, that they still refuse to let me go to Lady Pembroke (the old countess), although everyone knows I am married to her, but what is worst of all is that infamous scoundrel Halford was by at the marriage, and has now the effrontery to deny it to my face!'[4] The ever-scheming Prince of Wales rather hoped it might be true too, since he would be able to 'govern the King through her'. It was not, so he did not, but a greatly perturbed Betty

---

1   Herbert, *The Pembroke Papers*, I, p. 216.
2   Herbert, *Pembroke Papers*, II, pp. 259-60.
3   *ODNB*, 'Elizabeth Spencer'.
4   *Salisbury and Winchester Journal* (hereafter *SWJ*), 7 June 1856, quoting the Duke of Buckingham's *Court of Regency*. Sir Henry Halford (1766-1844) was President of the Royal College of Physicians.

offered to resign her place. The offer was refused, so she fell back on her well-honed skill for diplomacy in personal affairs. When George recovered from his first serious bout of madness in 1789 she wrote to him saying that 'Your majesty has always acted by me as the kindest brother as well as the most gracious of sovereigns … if I might presume to say that I felt like the most affectionate sister towards an indulgent brother it would exactly express my sentiments'.[1] It was testimony to Betty and Queen Charlotte that both accompanied the King to Weymouth that summer during which time the former behaved, according to the courtier Mrs Harcourt, 'with such propriety that her visit, which was much dreaded, proved most serviceable'.[2] The King's passions revived in 1804 when he suffered another 'episode' but the fact that he and the object of his infatuation were now septuagenarians meant, thanks to Betty's continuing tact, that gossip of the salacious variety, was avoided.

Countess Betty was finally released from her marital travails when, following a stroke, Earl Henry died, aged 59, in January 1794. Her son George, now 11th Earl, could embark on the task of getting the Wilton estate back in order whilst simultaneously pursuing an army career and raising a young family. It was, inevitably, the third task to which he could devote least time. No less inevitably it was Betty, his mother and now doting grandmother, who helped fill the void. It was a task all the more necessary following the death of the 11th Earl's first wife in 1793.

Dowager Betty herself was to enjoy considerable longevity. This carried a price in that she lived to see the passing of many of those dearest to her: Lady Di, her sister, died in August 1808; George, her son, and 11th Earl, died in October 1827. But there were the compensations of having seen him contract a happy second marriage to Catherine Woronzow in January 1808, the

1   *ODNB*, 'Elizabeth Herbert'.
2   *ODNB*, 'Elizabeth Herbert'. Alan Bennett's 1991 stage play, *The Madness of George III* (even more so the 1994 film version 'The Madness of King George'), uses a large amount of artistic licence in portraying Betty as a young seductress.

birth of their six children (their son Sidney, her grandson, was born at Pembroke Lodge, Richmond, in September 1810), and the marriage of her favourite granddaughter, Diana, in 1816. She became, by virtue of not having died herself, one of the grandest old ladies in society. Aged 70, she appeared at the Queen's birthday ball in 1807 in 'A superb dress of brown and silver; the petticoat richly embroidered in antique, and ornamented with silver fringe; brown crape train, elegantly ornamented with silver; head-dress brown and silver, with a profusion of diamonds'.[1] In the spring of 1815 it transpired that she had defied even the Grim Reaper: 'We have great satisfaction', reported the *Salisbury Journal*, 'in stating, that the article announcing the death of the Dowager Countess of Pembroke, inserted in several of the London papers, is totally unfounded; her Ladyship being this time in perfect health'.[2] Her tenure as a Lady of the Bedchamber only came to an end with the death of Queen Charlotte in November 1818. By then they had corresponded as close friends for forty years.

Betty finally died at the grand old age of 94 on April 30th 1831. She was buried in St Mary's, Wilton, with her son and daughter.[3] She had been Countess for 37 years, a record only subsequently beaten by Beatrice Paget in the twentieth century; and Dowager Countess for 38 years, a figure exceeded only by her predecessor, Henriette de Kérouaille. But Betty Spencer's life should not be reduced to statistics. It should be celebrated as that of a remarkable woman. Few put it better than the French hostess Marie Anne de Vichy-Chamrond, Maquise du Deffand: 'I like her Ladyship very much; the more I see her, the more I like her; her simplicity, her unaffected manner, her gentleness, her modesty are all informed by a keen intelligence; she is animated, without being vivacious, her opinions are well-founded ... [in short] she has the manners of an extremely noble woman.'[4]

1   *SWJ*, 8 June 1807.
2   *SWJ*, 8 May 1815.
3   *SWJ*, 16 May 1831. The bodies were moved to the Pembroke vault in the new church in Wilton in 1851.
4   Herbert, *The Pembroke Papers*, I, p. 37.

Elizabeth Beauclerk

F EW EVENTS IN Betty's Spencer's life as Countess of Pembroke
afforded her greater pleasure than the news that her son,
George Augustus, was to marry her niece (Lady Diana Spencer's
younger daughter by her second marriage), Elizabeth Beauclerk.
Elizabeth's paternal lineage brought royal blood into the Pembroke
family: she was the great-great granddaughter of Charles II and
his self-styled Protestant whore, Nell Gwyn. Although she would
not live to be Lady Pembroke (she was the fourth and penultimate
woman to have married an heir to the title who never became
Countess), Elizabeth was one of the select band of fourteen
women who gave birth to a future Earl of Pembroke.[1]

We know relatively little of Elizabeth Beauclerk beyond
that she was born in March 1769 and schooled for a while at
Campden House in Kensington.[2] But Countess Betty was fond
of her niece and, as we have seen, was living increasingly away
from Wilton in Richmond Park. There was therefore ample
opportunity for Elizabeth, living in reduced circumstances with
her widowed mother in Richmond after 1780, to get to know
her cousin George Augustus, future 11th Earl of Pembroke.
A decade older, George Augustus can have experienced only
'brotherly' feelings for her before the mid-1780s and in any case
he had his heart set on another cousin, Caroline Spencer, Lady
Sunderland, as a possible future Lady Pembroke. But his love
went unrequited.[3]

1   Since Robert, 12th Earl, did not sire a legitimate male heir, the royal
blood line at Wilton ended with his death in 1862.
2   Hicks, *Improper Pursuits*, pp. 200, 238. The author dates Elizabeth's
birth to March 1769, 'a respectable twelve months after the wedding'.
Other sources put the birth at 1768 or earlier.
3   Hicks, *Improper Pursuits*, pp. 298-9.

17. Elizabeth Beauclerk by Sir William Beechey, 1789

Elizabeth's was, however, unquestionably a love match. When George Augustus, with some trepidation, broke the news of his intentions to his father, the 10th Earl, he wrote that 'I have at last found one with whom I am confident I shall be happy, & who is of the same opinion of her side … & who so thoroughly approves of me'. The impecunious Earl Henry would have been even happier if his son 'had ye found a thirty thousand pounder as agreeable to ye as Elizabeth' but he could not gainsay her good character.[1] Although Elizabeth was not as penniless as has been

1   Herbert, *The Pembroke Papers*, II, pp. 340-1.

claimed, George was obviously what the contemporary writer, Lady Louisa Stuart, called 'a prodigious match for her'. The two were married in a quiet ceremony on April 8th 1787.[1]

Although Elizabeth suffered from indifferent health and George Augustus was sometimes away on military service, the marriage proved a happy one. A son, George, was born in 1788, followed by two further siblings, Diana and Robert, in 1790. Another son, Charles, entered the world on March 9th 1793, but Elizabeth departed from it suddenly, aged just 24, on March 25th. We can only presume that it had something to do with her final pregnancy. Her husband was grief struck, the more so when both baby Charles and George, his eldest son, died before the year was out. Little did he but know it, the future 11th Earl's surviving son, Robert, later 12th Earl, would give him further cause for grief a generation later. It was Diana who became the cynosure of his and Grandmother Betty's affections.[2] Diana survived to become a countess in her own right through her marriage to Welbore Ellis Agar, 2nd Earl of Normanton. Since the Normanton family seat was Somerley Park near Ringwood, only twenty miles from Wilton, she was able to maintain her local associations: her eldest son, James, sat as MP for the borough during the 1840s.

1   Hicks, *Improper Pursuits*, pp. 297-301; Herbert, *The Pembroke Papers*, II, p. 321.
2   Lever, *Herberts of Wilton*, p. 196; Herbert, *The Pembroke Papers*, II, p. 486.

CATHERINE WORONZOW

C ATHERINE WORONZOW was special.[1] Encouraged by his
father, in January 1787, to consider marrying a foreign
heiress, George Augustus, the future 11th Earl, had demurred:
'My objections to a foreign wife, I hope, will never cease. Let her
be perfection, her husband must be immediately connected with
a pack of foreigners, her country people, relations, & friends,
& that would never do'.[2] At the time, 1,800 miles away in St
Petersburg, Yekaterina Semyonovna Vorontsova was little more
than three years old. Born on October 24th 1783, she came to
England in 1785 when her father, Count Simon Woronzow, was
appointed his country's ambassador to Britain. He retired in 1806
and lived near Lord's Cricket Ground in North London until he
died in 1832. By then his daughter, 'the Russian Countess', had
long since been a star in the firmament of British society.

George Augustus, the 11th Earl, a good friend of the
Ambassador, had been widowed for nearly fifteen years when he
married Catherine, 24 years his junior, on January 26th 1808.
There were actually two ceremonies. The first took place in the
Greek Chapel in Marylebone according to the rites of the Greek
Orthodox Church. It was followed by a second service at the
Dowager Countess Betty's house in Cavendish Square where a
special licence for the purpose had been granted to John Fisher,
Bishop of Salisbury.[3] Although a few eyebrows were raised at the

1   This is the name by which she is best known at Wilton today. The
usual Russian spelling of the name is Voronotsov. Within the family
she was known variously as Tish, Kat, Katrina, Katinka, and Mammy.
She signed herself as 'Catherine Pembroke & Montgomery' on her son's
wedding certificate.
2   Herbert, *Pembroke Papers*, II, pp. 326-7.
3   *SWJ*, 1 Feb. 1808.

18. Catherine Woronzow by Sir Thomas Lawrence, c. 1809

difference in the newlyweds' age, and a few more at the bride's nationality, those in the know considered the match an admirable one. The young Viscount Palmerston informed friends that the wedding had 'given great pleasure to all her [Catherine's] friends. Ld Pembroke is certainly a good deal older than she is, but her habits are more formed than those of most young women of her age, and he bears his years lightly, and as they have been intimate from her childhood the objection is not strong'.[1]

1   Foster, *Sidney Herbert*, pp. 18-19.

It was November 1808 before Catherine first visited Wilton as its new chatelaine. In June 1810 Parliament passed an Act to naturalise her as a British subject.[1] But it did not need a change in the law to demonstrate that she could fulfil the roles of an English countess. By 1819 Catherine had produced five daughters, all of whom would make propitious marriages.[2] There was also a son, Sidney, by whose sons she would become grandmother to two future Earls of Pembroke. Locally, Catherine agreed to be patron of Salisbury's Race Ball and its Music Festival. On the Wilton estate, in January 1821, 'The Countess of Pembroke has been very bountiful, at this season, in donations of coal and clothing to the needy poor of Bishopstone'.[3] Through her mother-in-law, the Dowager Countess Betty, she was soon corresponding with the elderly Queen Charlotte.[4] In her own right she proved a more than adequate hostess. The Grand Duke Nicholas, later Czar Nicholas I, visited Wilton in 1817: the tree he planted still stands. Just before Christmas 1819, British royalty called in the persons of the Duke and Duchess of Kent with their five month old daughter Alexandrina, the future Queen Victoria.[5]

The Earl may reasonably have counted on Catherine being able to discharge the essentially traditional roles of Countess as outlined above. What he probably did not know, though it was serendipitous, was that he had married a 'project manager'. Nearly a decade before Catherine entered Wilton's portals, George Augustus had embarked on the most ambitious reconfiguration of the house since the creation of the State Apartment in the South wing during the reign of Charles I.

1   *SWJ*, 11 Nov. 1808, 25 June 1810.
2   Elizabeth (b.1809), married Richard, 3rd Earl Clanwilliam; Mary (b.1813), married George, 2nd Marquess of Ailesbury; Catherine (b. 1814), married Alexander, 6th Earl of Dunmore; Georgiana (b.1817), married Henry, 4th Marquess of Lansdowne; Emma (b.1819), married Thomas, 3rd Viscount de Vesci.
3   *SWJ*, 9 Aug. 1819, 29 Jan. 1821, 23 Aug. 1824.
4   Herbert, *Pembroke Papers*, II, p. 500.
5   *SWJ*, 3 Mar. 1817, 27 Dec. 1819. Victoria visited Wilton House again in 1832 en route to Salisbury from Edington.

Although content with the latter, the Earl objected to much else; succinctly put, he sought 'to give a large house the comfort and convenience of a small one'. To this end, in 1801, he engaged James Wyatt to overhaul the North and West wings, to move the main entrance from the East to the North side (in the process adding a new North forecourt), and insert corridors within the quadrangle of the original building. But Wyatt, for all his prestige as the leading architect of the age, was constrained by the huge amount of work that came with his meteoric rise to fame. By nature insouciant, once the plan had been agreed, he rarely put in an appearance at Wilton. Given that his deputies proved ineffective, and that diplomatic duties caused the Earl to be away more than he would have liked, it was not entirely surprising that the work stalled. Worse, some glaring examples of defective workmanship were discovered. With the bills having mushroomed to £50,000 (equivalent to over £4,000,000 at current values), an exasperated Earl terminated Wyatt's contract in 1810.[1]

If the young Countess (just turned 27 when Wyatt was sent packing) was not quite literally left to pick up the pieces, it did fall largely to her to oversee a local builder, Money Fisher, and the sculptor, Richard Westmacott, in making good and completing the alterations to the main fabric of the building. It was, however, in the subsequent arranging, decorating and furnishing of the house that she was really given licence to employ her manifold talents. The most pressing need, during the 1810s, was to do something about the family's prized collection of antique sculptures (nearly 200 pieces), 'thrown about', according to a visitor in 1810, 'higgledy-piggledy, sans nose, sans fingers, sans every other prominent member from a field of battle'. Under her supervision, the principal pieces were rearranged around the newly-finished Cloisters: 'The Countess determined the precise positions of the sculptures with careful consideration of their significance and picturesque effect'. The numbers she allocated

1　Robinson, *Wilton House*, pp. 172-95.

19. Wilton House, North Cloister

to them became a sort of unofficial inventory, an indispensable
starting point for all serious academic research since.[1]

Next to claim the Countess's attention were the renovated
rooms leading off the Cloisters. Whilst it was Westmacott who
was responsible for much of the practical work required, he did
so only after his sketches had received her official endorsement.

1   Stewart, *Sculpture Collection*, p. 37.

*20. The Double Cube Room, displaying some of Catherine Woronzow's
furniture, with van Dyck's great family portrait on the far wall (see figure 8)*

Those who doubt it can read Catherine's annotations (her hand,
be warned, is demanding!) for themselves. They include strictures
such as 'too crowded' and 'not proper'; and listings of dimensions
for curtains and the like.[1] So far as furniture was concerned – there
had been surprisingly little in the State Apartment before this time

1   Robinson, *Wilton House*, pp. 207, 211.

21. The Italian Garden, West side of Wilton House (author's collection)

22. The Church of Saint Mary and Saint Nicholas, Wilton
(author's collection)

23. The Palladian Bridge, 1737 (author's collection)

– Catherine's eye and taste were revealed in the purchase of gilt and crimson settees, easy chairs, and sofas by William Kent acquired at the dispersal sale of goods from Wanstead House in Essex in 1822. These were supplemented by newly commissioned pieces in the same style. Further items obtained, with which to adorn the State Apartment and other rooms, included clocks, Boulle tables, and a gilt fire screen said to have been spirited from Versailles in the aftermath of the French Revolution. At the same time the Countess was also using Westmacott to execute stone seats, bridges and loggia in the Park, whilst an orangery was erected alongside her piece de resistance, the Italian garden, immediately to the west of the house.[1] Whilst it is debatable, as has recently been asserted, that Catherine was 'the most forceful of the of the early chatelaines of Wilton,' it is certainly true that none has effected such a visible and long lasting set of changes to its interior décor and gardens.[2]

Catherine's work had not long been completed when her husband died, aged 68, on October 26th 1827. In normal

1   Robinson, *Wilton House*, pp. 202-204.
2   Russell, *Pictures and Drawings at Wilton House*, p. 154.

circumstances, Catherine would now have left Wilton to make way for Robert, 12th Earl, and his Countess, and fade into relative obscurity. She was, after all, only the new Earl's stepmother, had rarely, if ever, met him, and can hardly have entertained a positive view of him, formed as it must have been, by her late husband who regarded Robert as a wastrel who had rushed into an unsuitable marriage. There is a story in the family that, apprised of Robert's supposed failings, Catherine deposited a box of gems (once belonging to Cardinal Mazarin and bought by the Pembrokes in the eighteenth century), at Hoare's bank in order to prevent Robert from selling them and frittering away the proceeds.[1] She also appears, in the short term anyway, to have left Wilton for London.

Circumstances, however, were not normal; the truth more nuanced. Whilst it was true that Robert and the 11th Earl had long been estranged, that his marriage had proved disastrous, and that he had lived abroad for many years, he was also amiable and easy going. He evinced no strong desire to assume the reins at Wilton and had no reason to dislike a 44 year old Dowager only eight years his senior. Quite apart from being too young to do so, Catherine was too vivacious a character to contemplate 'retirement'. And she had, of course, only had a few years to enjoy the Wilton in which she had invested so much. It made good sense all round therefore, for Earl Robert to rent Wilton to Catherine and her children.[2] Thus it was that the 'inmates' as the *Salisbury Journal* quaintly put it, arrived 'home' on November 13th 1834: 'On Thursday last, the Dowager Countess of Pembroke and the Ladies Herbert arrived at Wilton Abbey, to take up their residence, highly to the gratification of the inhabitants. The various clubs assembled on the occasion, and marched with their banners and an excellent band of music to the Abbey'.[3]

---

1   Stewart, *Sculpture Collection*, p. 19. They were last sighted in 1911 when the bank rediscovered them. Ironically, the financially straitened 15th Earl probably disposed of them soon afterwards.

2   *SWJ*, 20 Oct. Sept. 1834.

3   *SWJ*, 20 Oct., 17 Nov. 1834.

Neither did Catherine abandon her position in London society. She maintained the lease on the 11th Earl's address in Stanhope Street, if only to keep his Tory political circle intact for the benefit of her politically aspiring son, Sidney.[1] At the end of 1832, however, Prince Michael Woronzow, her brother, spent £10,000 in order for her to acquire the lease on 1, Grafton Street, one of the most exclusive addresses in Mayfair; she took a villa at Norwood pending its redecoration.[2]

The Dowager Catherine was thereby enabled to continue her roles as benefactress and patron. At Christmas 1834, the poor of Wilton were gifted blankets, coal, potatoes and beef. As the decade proceeded, her name, even if she did not always appear in person, was attached to events such as the Salisbury Dahlia Show and a ball or two in the City's Assembly Rooms.[3] She interspersed these activities with periods of foreign travel (Frankfurt in 1836, Paris in 1837, Nice for the winter of 1839-40, for example), and playing the hostess at home.[4] At Wilton, guests during the summer of 1837 included Princess Maria Augusta of Saxony, and Count Pyotr Tolstoy; her brother, Prince Michael, joined her there in 1838.[5] Her greatest coup of the decade, however, was the Grand Ball given in Grafton Street, in May 1839, for the Grand Duke Alexander (later Czar Alexander II), 'attended by a great number of the leading nobility and gentry at present in the metropolis ... Dancing commenced shortly before twelve o'clock ... A sumptuous supper was laid out in the large drawing-room for 150 persons'.[6]

---

1   *SWJ*, 28 May 1832; Lord Stanmore, *A Memoir of Sidney Herbert*, I, p. 17.
2   *SWJ*, 4 June, 26 Nov. 1832, 29 July 1833. Michael Woronzow (1782-1856), 'heir to 24,000 souls', was well-known in Britain. He had been prominent in Russia's war against Napoleon (he presented one of the Emperor's despatch cases to Wilton House) and later rose to become Governor-General in the Caucasus and a Prince of Russia.
3   *SWJ*, 29 Dec. 1834, 2 Oct. 1837, 14 Jan. 1839.
4   *SWJ*, 14 Nov. 1836, 6 Feb. 1837, 18 Nov. 1839.
5   *SWJ*, 28 Aug., 23 Oct. 1837, 5 Nov. 1838.
6   *SWJ*, 3 June 1839.

Much the same pattern continued during the first half of the 1840s: roughly speaking, Catherine went abroad (German spa towns were a favoured destination), for the winter, returned to London for 'the season', and came down to Wilton during the summer. An exception was when Prince Michael came for a much-publicised stay of nearly six months from the late summer of 1843; the undoubted highlight was the visit of Czar Nicholas I to Grafton Street in June 1844. Grand Duke Constantine, his second son, paid his respects in 1847.[1]

Lest the reader think otherwise, however, Catherine's attentions were never exclusively devoted to her own entertainment. It was religion (she told her son that 'she had always put her whole faith and trust in God ... from a child'), far more than interior design, that was the real driving passion in her life.[2] One of many churches to benefit, she gave money for the repair of Little Bedwyn church, near Marlborough, in 1842. The same year she subscribed the considerable sum of £200 (roughly £20,000 at current monetary values) towards making possible the employment of a full time chaplain at Salisbury Infirmary.[3]

It is in Wilton itself, however, that the most notable example of Catherine's commitment to good works can still be seen. The medieval parish church of St Mary's had reached the stage where replacement seemed preferable to restoration. In face of that dilemma, in July 1839, it was announced that she, in tandem with her son, Sidney, would finance the building of a new one. Pembroke land was assigned accordingly; building began in the spring of 1841.[4] Catherine's personal contribution can be identified most obviously in the decision to erect the structure along a north-south alignment, the Russian Orthodox custom, as opposed to the usual Anglican norm of an east-west axis. She

---

1   *SWJ*, 19 Aug., 30 Sept., 7 Oct. 1843, 8, 15 June 1844, 29 May 1847. The Czar paid a second visit to bid farewell before he returned to Russia.
2   Stanmore, *Sidney Herbert*, II, p. 36.
3   *SWJ*, 28 Mar. 1842, 21 Jan. 1843.
4   *SWJ*, 29 July 1839, 31 May 1841.

was also, surely, responsible for the Russian oak which framed the west doors, and certainly so for the high ornate pulpit of Caen stone with its Cosmato columns and supports of Spanish marble. Parts of the chancel too, it was reported, were to be paved 'with small squares agate, lava, and precious stones, collected abroad by the Countess of Pembroke'.[1] By the time the new church of St Mary and St Nicholas was consecrated on 9 October 1845, mother and son had lavished well over £60,000 on their grand design. Catherine paid for a grand party in the town to celebrate the occasion. Whilst Sidney Herbert is today afforded the greater credit as founder of the church the modern visitor might do well to reflect that contemporaries deemed it appropriate to erect monuments of equal size and prominence to mother and son on either side of the chancel.[2]

The infirmities of old age meant that Catherine's name appeared only rarely in the press after 1848. She was present at Wilton in September 1853, however, when the Grand Duchess Maria, daughter of Czar Nicholas I, was the guest of honour.[3] A year later such a gathering would have been impolitic, if not impossible: British soldiers were about to engage Russian ones in the Crimea. Catherine had gained popularity in her youth as the representative of a nation making common cause in war against Napoleon. In old age, as a daughter from a renowned military family now arraigned against her adopted country, commonsense, as well as advancing years rendered it expedient to maintain a low profile.

Catherine visited Wilton for the last time over Christmas 1855. Labouring 'with a constant and harassing cough … The day she went away … she stopped in the cloister [she had done so much to create] and looked round, saying, 'Ah! I never shall see this dear old place again!'[4] She died, aged 72, at her Grafton Street

1   *St Mary and St Nicholas Church Wilton. A Church Guide, passim*; *SWJ*, 1 Feb.1845.
2   *SWJ*, 11, 18 Oct. 1845; Foster, *Sidney Herbert*, pp. 160-2.
3   *SWJ*, 24 Sept. 1853.
4   Stanmore, *Sidney Herbert*, II, p. 35.

home on March 27th 1856. The fact that peace had not yet been concluded between Britain and Russia explains why the passing of such a remarkable lady was marked in the national press with only scant notice.[1] Wilton thought and acted differently: 'Since the intelligence of the death of this truly noble lady was received in this place there has been one universal feeling of sorrow, every house and shop being partially closed, as demonstration of the deep sympathy felt by the inhabitants in the melancholy event; indeed to them the loss is almost a personal one, as her amiability, courtesy, and benevolence had endeared her to every class, and while the poor of Wilton had for many years enjoyed her personal attention and liberal assistance, in every case of distress, given so unostentatiously that it was known only to the recipients, her charities were dispensed annually in every parish on the extensive Pembroke estates'.[2] When her coffin reached Wilton House from London on April 2nd, over 700 people filed past it in the entrance hall. There was, as her son was given pause to observe, 'much feeling shown'. The following morning, 'a day of tempest and rain … a vast number of people reverently followed my mother's coffin to the grave'. The main body of 28 family mourners, was followed, unusually for England, by sixteen men and women from the Wilton estate, all mentioned by name, who had served Catherine in life. She was buried in the family vault of her church alongside her husband, the 11th Earl.[3] Nearly forty years later, the passions of the war now having long subsided, William Gladstone, the Prime Minister, reflected sagely that Catherine 'was really of herself a kind of bond between the two countries'.[4]

1   *SWJ*, 29 Mar. 1856.
2   *SWJ*, 5 Apr. 1856.
3   *SWJ*, 5 Apr. 1856; Stanmore, *Sidney Herbert*, II, pp. 35-38.
4   Pembroke Papers, 2057/F4/60, Gladstone to Lady Herbert, 13 Jan. 1893.

Princess Octavia Spinelli

Visitors to Wilton will find no trace of Octavia Spinelli, and precious little of her husband, Robert 12th Earl. Viewed from the perspective of the descent of the Pembroke title, this is perhaps understandable, since their union produced no children. Yet it seems only fair in a book of this nature to re-integrate Octavia into the family story.[1] We cannot say much, but she was certainly more than 'the Countess who never was'.

Octavia was born in Italy, probably late in 1779. She was the daughter of Vincenzo Spinelli, Duke of Laurino, a Sicilian nobleman. Around the turn of the century she married Prince Ercole Branciforte de Butari. Although Octavia had a daughter by him, Butari was a good deal older than she was. Neither was he blessed with good health: it is tempting to suppose that she tired of him. At all events, her 35 year old head was turned by the 22 year old Robert, Lord Herbert, the only surviving son of Elizabeth Beauclerk and the 11th Earl, when he arrived in Palermo in 1814. Robert was 'introduced by Lady William Bentinck into the family of the Prince de Butari, whose palace was the great resort of all the English Nobility who visited that country, and who were always received with the Utmost hospitality'. He became an ever-present fixture in their entourage, and 'sedulously endeavoured to gain the favourable opinion of the Princess'. It was not long before he was being referred to as her *cavaliere servente*.[2] Mutual professions of love followed, with more to follow if and when the Prince died. This, though there were no suspicions of foul play, happened conveniently soon, in June. Octavia married her aristocratic toy boy on August 17th.

1 Lever, *Herberts of Wilton*, pp. 205-7, seemingly ignoring his own argument, is ambivalent about Octavia's status.
2 *Exeter Flying Post*, 6 May 1819.

News of the marriage was sufficiently sensational that it was soon being referred to in gossipy letters from English travellers abroad.[1] For the 11th Earl, however, word of what was impending spelt horror. Mindful of the family's reputation in wake of what he regarded as a mésalliance – not least because Octavia was a Roman Catholic – and the hurt his father's philandering had caused to his mother (Betty), George Augustus set off hot foot for Italy.[2] He arrived too late to prevent the wedding but drew some comfort from the fact that the banns had not, as would normally have been the case, been published. After taking advice, the Earl also sought to exploit a dated legal procedure whereby minors contracting an illicit marriage could be imprisoned for up to five years. In consequence, on August 21st, Octavia was arrested and confined for several months in a convent. Her husband, who found the curtailing of his freedom unappealing, decided that discretion was the better part of valour, and returned briefly to England in December 1814.[3]

Octavia, though we can only imagine the feelings she experienced, would soon discover that this was but the beginning of her ordeal. Subsequent reports said that persons of 'very high authority' (the insinuation was that it was the Earl) had tried to persuade Pope Pius VII and King Louis XVIII of France to bring pressure to bear in order to get the marriage annulled.[4] In fact it was Robert, a living exemplar of the adage 'marry in haste and repent at your leisure', who took the lead in what followed; and it was in the English courts that the story was most fully played out.

In order to contest the case Octavia came to England with

1   https://discovery.nationalarchives.gov.uk/details/r/6758cdb4-3246-4854-a55a-5c7c31323383d, Lady Emily James to her mother, Lady Londonderry, 5 Oct. 1814, accessed 15 Mar. 2022.
2   Anti-Catholicism was still a potent force in England, witness the Herbert family's aversion to Lady Herbert of Lea's conversion half a century later. The 11th Earl had come of age in 1780, the year of the Gordon riots when anti-Catholic mobs rampaged through London and up to 700 people had been killed.
3   Lever, *Herberts of Wilton*, p. 206.
4   *SWJ*, 10 Dec. 1827.

her brother, the Duke de Spinelli, in March 1817. However, it would be another two years before the case would be adjudicated upon. In the interim she took a house in Stratford Place, styled herself Lady Herbert, and was evidently accepted in fashionable London society. She is listed, for example, as being present at a soirée in the Marchioness of Lansdowne's home, in Albemarle Street, at the beginning of 1818.[1]

Legal proceedings had been started by the Herberts in 1815. The case against Octavia was that her marriage was invalid according to Sicilian law 'by reason of informality in the solemnisation', essentially that the ceremony had taken place clandestinely.[2] English courts first referred the case to the authorities in Palermo in order that witnesses – 39 of them – might be examined. This was duly done. But in February 1819, at the Consistory Court in England, Robert Herbert objected that their testimony should be ruled inadmissible on the grounds that they had not been examined in private. Octavia objected to the objection, the English courts found in her favour, and the evidence, 'which is of an interesting nature', was cleared to be heard on another day.[3]

The main case, Octavia's suit for the restitution of her conjugal rights, came before the court on April 30th.[4] Witness testimony having established the identity of Octavia and Lord Robert, the pivotal evidence was provided by the priest who had officiated at their union. He swore that 'the marriage was ... solemnized ... according to the rites of the Roman Catholic Church of Sicily'. The presiding judge, Sir William Scott, consequently ruled that since neither party was a minor, Octavia 'although somewhat older than [Robert] was yet not of an age which of itself implied any incongruity in the match', had made her case.[5] 'It was

---

1   *Morning Post*, 14 Jan. 1818.
2   *Morning Post*, 6 Feb. 1819.
3   *Morning Post*, 6 Feb. 1819. The Consistory Court, an ecclesiastical court, was superseded by the Divorce Court in 1857.
4   *Exeter Flying Post*, 6 May 1819.
5   Sir William Scott (1745-1836), created Lord Stowell in 1821.

established by law', he continued', 'that if a marriage was valid in the country where it took place, according to the rites and usages of that country, it was a good one here'. Sir William concluded by ordering Robert to pay costs and 'to receive [Octavia] as his wife with conjugal affection' before October. There was little chance of the latter: Herbert was reported to have been living abroad since 1815.

Octavia, who had at least won the essential point, returned to Italy. She received a douceur of sorts from the 11th Earl; it was reported to have risen to £2,000 per annum by the end of the 1820s.[1] She was referred to in the British press as the 'new countess' when Robert succeeded to the earldom in 1827 but the only references to her thereafter identify her as living with her brother, the Duke, in Sicily and as a lady at the Neapolitan Court.[2] Robert's account books reveal that she was receiving payments of £1,200 per annum during the 1840s, and probably beyond.[3]

Octavia died, aged 77, at her home in the Strada di Chiaza in Naples, on July 31st 1857. There was little public notice of her passing in England. An exception was the *Illustrated London News*. In its review of the eminent persons who had died that year, she was reasonably referred to as the Princess Countess of Pembroke.[4]

Shunned by the Pembroke family, Octavia never visited Wilton. The facts remain that she was the only princess to have married an Earl of Pembroke, and only the third foreigner to have done so. She was married to an Earl (or future Earl) for 42 years, longer than all but one of her counterparts, and was Countess for just a few months short of 30 years, longer than all but two of her predecessors and successors. It suited many in the family to think that as Robert had separated from her, and that Octavia had retired to live at home, the marriage somehow did not count as

1   *Morning Advertiser*, 15 Sept. 1829.
2   *SWJ*, 10 Dec. 1827, 17 Dec. 1838; *Illustrated London News*, 19 Dec. 1857.
3   Pembroke Papers 2057/A6/61.
4   *Illustrated London News*, 19 Dec. 1857.

real. But it was. The fact that the family did not expend the time, trouble and expense required to bring in a Bill of Parliament in an attempt to formalise a divorce shows that they knew so too.

Part 2
Dynasts and Others *c*.1846-1973

C ASUAL OBSERVERS COULD be forgiven for thinking that all seemed well in Wilton's world in 1851. The Herberts were celebrating 300 years as Earls of Pembroke; the title had passed seamlessly from father to son over five generations since 1683; their house was thrown open to visitors on Wednesdays and Fridays; and they happily footed the bill for over 400 people from the town to broaden their horizons by taking the train to the Great Exhibition at the Crystal Palace.[1] Scratch the surface, however, and there were grounds for anxiety. Robert, 12th Earl, was clearly going to have no son by Octavia Spinelli, but whilst she lived neither was he free to marry and father a legitimate heir by another woman. Aged 60 in 1851, his chosen lifestyle did not, in any case, augur well for Wilton's future. He was rarely in England after 1815, preferring instead to live in Paris whilst Catherine Woronzow and her children tenanted the family seat. This had worked well enough during the 1830s but relations became strained during the 1840s as reports of Robert's spiralling financial extravagances were compounded by prurient stories regarding his womanising.[2] He had two longstanding affairs. The first, with the dancer Alexina Gallott (c. 1839-1844), produced two sons and a daughter. His second, overlapping mistress, Marie Schöeffer (c.1842-1862), a Parisian dancer, produced two sons and two daughters. The latter paramour was a particular source of vexation to the Herbert family in England, who feared that Octavia's death would pave the way for the arrival of a French

---

1   Foster, *Sidney Herbert*, p. 160.
2   Foster, *Sidney Herbert*, pp. 141-3, 351-2.

countess at Wilton. Lizzie Herbert, one of those then domiciled at Wilton, wrote to William Gladstone fearing that her days there were numbered, 'how soon to be replaced we do not know, but there is no doubt by whom ... we have loved the dear old place too much'.[1]

The earldom itself, thanks to the various male progeny of Margaret Sawyer, was not especially imperilled.[2] But the senior branch of the Herbert line certainly was. In the unlikely event that Robert would bring a new chatelaine to Wilton and sire an heir, the earldom would pass to his half-brother Sidney, the only son of Catherine Woronzow and the 11th Earl. As heir apparent, Sidney had come under increasing pressure to marry since the early 1830s but resisted doing so until he was in his mid-thirties more than a decade later. It was well known, moreover, that his health was indifferent. The situation, however, was about to be retrieved with such spectacular success that its fruits still prosper at Wilton.

1   Gladstone Papers 44212, fols. 48-54, Elizabeth Herbert to Gladstone, 30 Aug. 1857.
2   Had Sidney Herbert not been born, Wilton and the Pembroke title would have passed to Henry Herbert, 4th Earl of Carnarvon, a great-great-great-grandson of Margaret Sawyer and the 8th Earl, on the death of the 12th Earl in 1862.

Elizabeth à Court

MARY ELIZABETH à COURT, or Lizzie as she was usually known, was born on July 21st 1822.[1] She was the only daughter of General Charles Ashe à Court, and Mary Elizabeth Gibbs. William, her uncle, became Lord Heytesbury and was variously British ambassador to Russia and Lord Lieutenant of Ireland. Her only sibling was a brother, Charles. Lizzie had a point when she wrote that 'I was brought up entirely amongst men'.[2]

Lizzie displayed an early flair for art. 'Her water-colour landscapes and representations of public buildings in Egypt and Palestine', read one assessment, 'are distinctly picturesque'. But art was almost a frivolous activity for a young woman so evidently earnest and industrious. Usually, 'she was the constant companion, and … the almost indispensable help, of her father … "fonder of work than of play."'[3]

The à Courts lived at Heytesbury House, barely fifteen miles from Wilton. They and the Herberts had long been close as families. Sidney Herbert, born in 1810, had known Lizzie since she was born. At the end of 1832 he visited the à Courts during his successful campaign to be returned as the Conservative Member of Parliament for South Wiltshire. According to Lizzie's governess, Sarah Hildyard, the ten year old Lizzie had said 'when looking out of the schoolroom window as he was riding away [...] "when I am a Woman, I will marry that man and no other!"'[4]

1 We refer to her here generally as Lizzie and as Lady Herbert from 1861 when her husband was ennobled.
2 *SWJ*, 4 Nov. 1911.
3 *Evening Mail*, 1 Nov. 1911.
4 Pembroke Papers 2057/F4/52, Hildyard to Elizabeth Herbert, 17 July 1846.

Whilst we can discard the above as the throw away remark of an impressionable young girl, we cannot so lightly dismiss the phalanx of evidence left by the men who encountered Lizzie a decade or so later. Palmerston wrote that Lizzie 'combined in an unusual degree Beauty that fascinates, warmth of heart that endears, and powers of intellect that assist and enliven'.[1] That intellect – friends dubbed her 'Lady Lightning' – caught the attention of Sir Robert Peel, leader of the Conservative Party. Lizzie recalled that Sir Robert, whose country seat in Staffordshire was next door to à Court family property at Amington Hall, 'took a fancy to me as a Pupil'. From the late 1830s Peel employed her as a part-time secretary, thereby broadening what Lizzie liked to call her 'political training'.[2] She reflected that the opportunity Peel afforded her had brought her into contact with a whole host of political luminaries, and that few women had 'lived in politics as she had ... I had always lived with and been treated as the equal and companion of clever men'.[3]

The news, made public in July 1846, that Lizzie would fulfil her childhood ambition by marrying Sidney Herbert was greeted with a chorus of approval. The wedding took place at St George's Church in Hanover Square on August 12th 1846; they reached Wilton for the first time as husband and wife on August 27th. As they approached the house they were 'preceded by young females, dressed in white, wearing chaplets of white roses, strewing flowers, to the gates of the Abbey'.[4] After thanking the hundreds who had gathered to greet them, 'we went out into the Garden & to the Palladian Bridge & there darling Sid, who was much moved, took both my hands & said to me – "you see how good these people are to me, darling. Will you help me to try more to deserve their love?"'[5] Lizzie herself was given pause to reflect that 'my new

1   Foster, *Sidney Herbert*, p. 454.
2   M. Bostridge, *Florence Nightingale*, p. 117.
3   Broadlands Papers GC/HE/105, Lady Herbert to Palmerston, 16 Oct. 1861; Lady Herbert, *How I Came Home*, pp. 3, 12.
4   *SWJ*, 29 Aug. 1846.
5   Pembroke Papers 2057/F4/49, Elizabeth Herbert to the Dowager Lady Pembroke, nd, Sept. 1846.

24. Lady Herbert of Lea with George, Lord Herbert and The Honourable Mary Herbert by Richard Thorburn, 1853

home had been St Edith's old monastery: so that it seemed as if she were to follow and form part of my life'.[1]

A rueful Peel had told Sidney on his engagement that 'you will gain a charming wife, but you will deprive me of the services of a most excellent secretary'. Lizzie was soon, of course, serving Herbert as secretary too, 'spending all her leisure writing letters and collecting material for the speeches in Parliament'.[2] The bedrock of the happy marriage which followed, however, was the couple's deeply held religious convictions which impelled them to

1 Herbert, *How I Came Home*, p. 4.
2 *SWJ*, 4 Nov. 1911.

do good works. At the time of his marriage to Lizzie, Sidney was best known in the wider world as a High Churchman (Anglo-Catholic). Lizzie's religious journey to the same destination, and ultimately beyond it, was more tortuous.

As a girl Lizzie had found 'utterly and entirely distasteful' a Sunday worship whose keynotes were 'cold and formal services, high pews, long puritanical hymns and intolerably dry sermons'.[1] During the 1830s, however, she had found 'life and warmth and practice' in the Oxford Movement, which reacted 'against the increasing secularisation of the Church of England, and sought to recall it to its heritage of apostolic order, and to the catholic doctrines of the early church fathers'.[2] Avidly devouring anything written by the Movement's leading lights (John Henry Newman and Henry Manning in particular), Lizzie concluded that she could best give practical expression to her faith by becoming a Sister of Charity, an order dedicated to the service of the poor. As a first step, she 'adopted' a village on the à Court's Warwickshire estate with no school and only the shell of a chapelry dedicated, by happy coincidence, to St Edith. Lizzie claimed, partly through selling some of her pictures, that she was able both to build a chancel and open a school. Her father, when he found out, fearing that her actions were symptomatic of a worrying drift away from the family's Protestant roots, immediately put a stop to her initiative.[3]

Lizzie's religious horizons were expanded, however, by her lengthy honeymoon tour of 1847-8. Much of the time was spent in Italy where visits to churches and monasteries, even attendance at Catholic Masses, became daily fare. She fell in love with the Eternal City: 'I don't know', she wrote prophetically, 'why one clings to Rome so much more than to any place which is not one's

---

1   Herbert, *How I Came Home*, p. 1.
2   Herbert, *How I Came Home*, p. 2; http://www.puseyhouse.org.uk/what-was-the-oxford-movement.html accessed 18 Jan. 2022.
3   Herbert, *How I Came Home*, pp. 2-3.

very own Home?'[1] Whilst there, her husband reintroduced her to his old Oxford acquaintance, Henry Manning. On first doing so, in autumn 1846, Sidney had styled Manning 'the holiest man I know'. In Lizzie's eyes Manning more than lived up to his billing.[2] 'I feel', she wrote to him in February 1848, 'as if there is a link between us wh. neither absence nor time could ever change or weaken ... there exists so wide a difference between you the tried & faithful servant & I the weak & vagabond child ... you have taught me much & done me much good. Pray for me'.[3]

Back at Wilton, from 1848, Lizzie was soon sharing in her husband's popularity as a paternalist landlord. Among the couple's more esoteric acts of charity was what Lizzie called *le plat du bon Jesu*. This involved taking leftover food from the house, perhaps 'the wing of a chicken or pheasant, or a cutlet with some nice vegetables; a slice of pudding, or pie or fruit', and presenting it to a family on the estate identified as being in need. Lizzie also displayed an interest in education by assuming responsibility for the running of a girls' school in Wilton Park, just a few hundred yards from the main house.[4] Proof positive that she took more than an employer's concern for the people working within it are a remarkable series of photographs (c. 1855) of several of their number annotated in her own hand. When the 83 year old Sarah Parham, housemaid at Wilton for 61 years, was fading in 1856, she summoned her husband down from Parliament to hold the dying woman's hand.[5]

The married Lizzie's broader sense of a religious mission for the poor was soon extending beyond the Herbert estates. She became a warm supporter of the Clewer House of Mercy, near

1   Manning Papers c. 657, fols 18-22, Elizabeth Herbert to Manning, 3 Apr. 1848.
2   Herbert, *How I Came Home*, pp. 4-5. Manning (1808-1892), a towering figure in the Oxford Movement, had been Archdeacon of Chichester since 1842.
3   Manning Papers c. 657, fols 6-11, Elizabeth Herbert to Manning, 22 Feb. 1848.
4   Foster, *Sidney Herbert*, pp. 159-60.
5   Stanmore Papers 49270, fol. 143.

25. Sarah (Sally) Parham, Head Housemaid at Wilton

Windsor. Clewer had been established under the auspices of the
Church of England in 1849 by Mariquita Tennant. It provided a
home for women identified as being at risk of falling into the twin
abysses of crime and prostitution. In writing to Tennant in 1850,
Lizzie confided that 'none are, I think, more pitiable than the
class of servants-of-all-work. I find that it is positively a common
thing for them to be engaged without wages or clothes and only

for food every other day. Who can wonder at girls so situated yielding to temptation and sin?'[1] She would back her words with both financial support and many visits over the coming years.

The philanthropic cause in which Lizzie played the most active part at mid-century, however, was emigration. Sidney had been much moved by the plight of slopworkers (young women making cheap clothing for nominal pay) during a visit to London's East End in December 1849.[2] He did not need Lizzie to tell him that they were just the sort of people whom circumstance might bring – a few lucky ones perhaps – to Clewer. Better for some of them, surely, to be encouraged to depart for the Antipodes? There were, after all, only 65,000 people living in New Zealand, and only 400,000 in Australia, and notably more men than women in both. Via the columns of the *Morning Chronicle*, the Herberts invited donations for what they decided to call the Female Emigration Fund.[3]

The Herberts threw themselves into fund raising. Solicitous letters yielded £500 from Queen Victoria and Prince Albert, a sum Lizzie and Sidney matched from their own pockets. Nearly £19,000 had been subscribed by the end of January 1850. Whilst it is true that Sidney bore the brunt of the resulting work by which the money was translated into placements in the colonies, he kept Lizzie actively involved throughout. She was, for instance, appointed chair of the committee to oversee the collection and distribution of clothing.[4]

Amid much publicity, the first emigrants left London on February 25th 1850. By year's end 409 emigrants had sailed in ten ships.[5] The Herberts made a point of trying to be present as each vessel departed. Lizzie was no mere ornament on such occasions. She spoke to some of the women about to leave and presented

1   V. Bonham, *The Founders of Clewer*, p. 22.
2   *Morning Chronicle*, 4 Dec. 1849.
3   *Morning Chronicle*, 5 Dec. 1849.
4   *The Times*, 4 Jan., 18 Feb., 16 Mar. 1850; *Morning Post*, 21 Apr. 1851.
5   *The Times*, 28 Feb. 1851.

all of them with addressed envelopes: 'Mrs Herbert hopes you will write to her as soon after your arrival as you can; she will be very anxious to know how you have got through the voyage, and whether you have got a place, and how you are getting on'.[1]

The Herberts' emigration project waned with time. Nevertheless, it was being reported, in June 1853, that 1,200 women had emigrated thanks to the £26,000 raised.[2] Thereafter the Fund probably merged with the broader based Family Loan and Colonisation Society.[3] During the time it had prospered, Lizzie and her husband were often mocked as 'do-gooders', scratching at the surface of the problem of overpopulation with their scheme for the 'mere shovelling out of paupers'.[4] To this they replied that 'because we cannot do everything, are we to do nothing … We may be pioneers for public opinion and ultimately for government assistance'.[5] Historians have been generous. The Female Emigration Fund was 'one of the most fashionable charities on the London scene … its favourable publicity contributed to the changing image of emigration'.[6] One can reasonably extrapolate that there must be tens of thousands of Australians and New Zealanders alive today descended in part from those who arrived there thanks to Lizzie and her husband. The present authors were on guide duty at Wilton House in 2018 when a member of the public introduced herself as being on a pilgrimage (her words) from New Zealand to see the home of the philanthropists whose initiative had enabled one of her female ancestors to cross the world in search of a better life a century and a half before.

One of the less onerous demands on Lizzie's time during the early 1850s was as a member of the management committee of the Institute for the Care of Sick Gentlewomen in Upper

1   *Morning Post*, 21 Apr. 1851, for Elizabeth Herbert's letter of 18 Apr.
2   Pembroke Papers 2057/F8/IX; *Morning Chronicle*, 11 June 1853.
3   *SWJ*, 29 Jan., 11 June, 13 Aug. 1853; *The Times*, 3 Nov. 1862.
4   Pembroke Papers 2057/F4/53, Lincoln to Sidney Herbert, 31 Jan. 1850.
5   Foster, *Sidney Herbert*, p. 174.
6   A. Hammerton, *Emigrant Gentlewomen*, ch. 4.

Harley Street. She was thus at least part responsible for securing the appointment of her friend, Florence Nightingale, as its superintendent in August 1853. A year later, with Sidney in government as Secretary at War, British troops landed in the Crimea. It soon became clear that they were enduring unnecessary hardships as a result of deficiencies in provision for the sick and wounded. The precise detail of who then spoke to whom will never be known, but Lizzie was certainly part of the conversation which resulted in Herbert issuing an invitation to Nightingale on behalf of the government (October 15th 1854) to take a party of nurses to Scutari. One surviving fragment, at least, suggests that some saw the part Lizzie played as being far more important than existing accounts allow. Signed 'M.S'., and dated October 1854, it reads: 'Now it is clear that there is something to do. You have certainly founded the whole thing & yr. Sid launched it'.[1]

Lizzie was certainly doing something. In the week from mid-October she chaired the small committee which interviewed those who had applied to join Nightingale's party. The interviews were held at her London home, 49 Belgrave Square. She was presumably present when Sidney addressed the assembled group of 38 in their dining room, prior to their departure, on October 20th.[2] Florence subsequently wrote to Lizzie as chair of the selection committee, detailing the progress of the nurses in her charge.[3]

As Nightingale's fame spread, Lizzie assisted Sidney in exploiting it for charitable ends. They rightly sensed that the British public wanted to commemorate 'the lady with the lamp'; they also knew that in peacetime she had spoken of setting up a training school for nurses. The result was the Nightingale Fund, launched in November 1855, which has been hailed as 'the first

---

1   Pembroke Papers 2057/F4/52. 'M.S'. is presumably Mary Stanley (1813-1879), nurse, philanthropist, and friend of the Herberts.
2   Bostridge, *Florence Nightingale*, pp. 207-9.
3   Foster, *Sidney Herbert*, p. 453.

national appeal in Britain aimed at all classes' of society.[1] With
Lizzie and Sidney in their element soliciting contributions from
the rich and famous, the Fund had reached £48,000 (well over
£5,000,000 today) by June 1857. The Nightingale Training
School for Nurses at St Thomas's Hospital in London opened in
June 1860.[2]

By then, Lizzie was embarked on a losing battle to save her
husband's life. Sidney was debilitated with Bright's disease, a
disease of the kidneys for which there was no effective treatment.
In an attempt to mitigate his parliamentary burdens, she persuaded
Palmerston to have him elevated to the House of Lords as Lord
Herbert of Lea.[3] Lizzie duly became Lady Herbert of Lea (as we
will now refer to her) on January 15th 1861. Little more than six
months later, however, on August 2nd 1861, Sidney was dead.
As her heart-wrenching account of their last days together bears
painful testimony, Lizzie's devotion was unstinting to the end.

One unedifying episode, born of Lady Herbert's
determination to lobby Palmerston during her husband's illness,
followed Sidney's death. Put bluntly, the Prime Minister became
infatuated with her. Married, and at 77 years old, 35 years Lady
Herbert's senior, the aged lothario imagined her as his secretary,
'that same secretary to be by my side every part of the four and
twenty hours'. He begged for a lock of her hair, 'a great treasure,
and your abundant tresses will not look the thinner or the scantier
for its being withdrawn from their amplitude'. Palmerston's
overtures were rejected in what the contrite Premier described as
a 'very angry letter', couched 'in somewhat strong language'.[4] The

1   Pembroke Papers 2057/F4/61, Sidney Herbert to Palmerston, 17
Oct. 1855; *The Times*, 30 Nov. 1855; M. Baly, *Florence Nightingale and
the Nursing Legacy*, p. 17.
2   S. Goldie (ed), *Florence Nightingale in the Crimean War*, pp. 184-5;
Baly, *Nursing Legacy*, ch. 2; Bostridge, *Florence Nightingale*, pp. 364-9,
428-31.
3   Since 1862, therefore, the Earl of Pembroke and Montgomery has
also been Lord Herbert of Lea.
4   Pembroke Papers 2057/F4/62, Palmerston to Lady Herbert, 21
Oct., 12 Nov. 1861.

letter has, understandably, not survived.

Lady Herbert was anyway too preoccupied with perpetuating her husband's memory to pursue the matter. A long poetic tribute to Sidney appeared under her initials in the *Salisbury Journal*.[1] She lent personal effects to the sculptor, Carlo Marochetti, who received the public commission to fashion the statue of Herbert which was dedicated in Salisbury's market square in June 1863.[2] Smaller memorials for which Lady Herbert paid from her own pocket included a window in Swallowcliffe church, ten miles west of Wilton in 1863. A generation later, she took considerable pains to ensure that a literary memorial to her husband appeared. Having flirted with writing it herself, the responsibility was entrusted to Lord Stanmore. Stanmore took more than a decade to complete his task, not least because when he presented what he hoped was the final draft, Lady Herbert objected that he had not been sufficiently revealing of Herbert's character. She assisted by sending him personal reminiscences. Much of the material was included verbatim by Stanmore when the book was finally published in 1906.[3]

Sidney's death was also the catalyst which cleared Lady Herbert's pathway to Roman Catholicism. Manning, her religious mentor, had made that journey in 1851.[4] For the sake of Sidney's political career, however (Catholics had only even been allowed to become MPs in 1829), Manning insisted that he and Lady Herbert should cease all contact. Lady Herbert, who had 'racking doubts', demurred, before acquiescing in Manning's logic. She then endured what she described as 'a sort of religious shipwreck' before resuming regular contact with him in 1863.[5] She formally converted, on January 5th 1865, at a private ceremony in a church

1   Foster, *Sidney Herbert*, p. 428.
2   R. E. Foster, 'Remembering Sidney Herbert: A Statuesque History', Sarum Chronicle, XX, 2020, pp. 7-22.
3   Foster, Sidney Herbert, pp. 442-5.
4   Manning became a cardinal in 1875.
5   Herbert, *How I Came Home*, pp. 5-7, 10. Manning was received into the Catholic Church on April 6th 1851.

at Palermo in Sicily. 'It is only when the step is taken', she wrote, 'that the full light bursts upon the soul, the scales seem to fall from one's eyes and one realises the eternal truth of the One Holy Catholic and Roman Church'.[1]

Lady Herbert was well aware that her conversion would come at a cost. Many Anglicans remained paranoid about Catholicism; she ruefully acknowledged, moreover, that none aroused greater suspicion than the zealous convert. She was quite prepared to incur 'the contempt and distrust of all people whose good opinion I most valued', but fearful 'of giving pain to so many that I love'.[2] The latter included her brother, Charles à Court-Repington, and Viscount de Vesci, her brother-in-law through marriage; they were especially worried at how the family's standing might be impacted if she schooled her four sons and three daughters in the Roman Catholic faith. Ignoring the instruction in Sidney's will that 'Lady Herbert is appointed sole guardian of the persons and estates of his children', they had them made wards of court.[3] Strict rules were laid down for their education and some restrictions on access to them were imposed on Lady Herbert. She did not need to be told in 1868 that it 'was a draught of bitterness for you, my dearest child, which you can only drink alone'.[4] The pain, thankfully, was shortlived. George, her eldest son, 13th Earl of Pembroke, came of age, an Anglican, in 1871. Lady Herbert had been allowed to accompany him to the West Indies in 1867 and had taken all the children on their annual foreign tour in the year following her conversion.[5]

Lady Herbert nevertheless remained popular at Wilton. She was cheered at the annual school festival in July 1868. At the harvest home festival two months later, 'taking the lead ... Her

1   Lady Herbert, *Anglican Prejudices Against the Catholic Church*, preface to 1899 edition.
2   Lady Herbert, *Anglican Prejudices Against the Catholic Church*, p. 45.
3   Pembroke Papers 2057/D5/13, will dated 10 July 1858.
4   R. St Lawrence, 'Lady Elizabeth Herbert of Lea, 1822-1911', *Sarum Chronicle*, I, 2001, pp. 40-41.
5   *SWJ*, 19 May 1866, 19 Oct. 1867.

ladyship, her sons and indeed all who joined in the procession, wore on their breasts large coloured rosettes surmounted with ears of wheat'.[1] In the wider locality Lady Herbert agreed to become patron of the Salisbury Mission. When St Osmund's Catholic Church in the city ran into financial difficulties she provided it with vessels, vestments, a new organ and £100 per annum. Lady Herbert also financed the building of a small school (1867) next door to the church in Exeter Street. Run by Sisters of Charity, it survived for 64 years.[2]

From the mid-1860s onwards Lady Herbert would reach a wider audience by putting her lifelong facility with the pen to good use.[3] By the time she died, with more than 30 titles to her name across a range of genres, she was by far Wilton's most prolific author since Mary Sidney. They included travel works such as *Impressions of Spain* (1866) and *Cradle Lands* (1867), religious tomes (often translations from the French), such as *Three Phases of Christian Love* (1867), and the semi-autobiographical *Edith* (a predictable choice of title!). There were also two pamphlets written for the Catholic Truth Society, which she helped to found in 1868.

But it was good works, not good books, which remained Lady Herbert's primary focus. Her essential ally during this last phase of her life was Herbert Vaughan. When she met him, in 1866, Vaughan was in the throes of setting up a training school for missionary priests in north London at Mill Hill. It was a project in which she joined with enthusiasm. Wealth and contacts were commodities of which Vaughan was in urgent need: Lady Herbert was well versed in tapping both. She did much to turn Vaughan's dream (he called her 'a wonderful beggar') into reality. St Joseph's Missionary Society of Mill Hill was formally established in June

1869. When working on the premises Lady Herbert stayed at a cottage in its grounds. She was also happy to host some of the society's meetings at her London home in Belgrave Square; she was, after all, honourary treasurer. Not for nothing did she earn the epithet 'The Mother of the Mill'.[1]

The more famous tangible memorial for which Lady Herbert can claim part credit is Westminster Cathedral, seat of the Catholic archbishop. Both she and Vaughan became driving forces of the project during the 1890s (Vaughan, who became a cardinal in 1893, had succeeded Manning as Archbishop of Westminster in 1892). The foundation stone was laid in 1895; the building opened in 1903, and was consecrated in June 1910.

Lady Herbert also continued to travel a great deal, visiting both the United States and Russia in her later years. But Rome remained her destination of choice. Though she usually celebrated Christmas in England, she spent nearly every winter in Rome for upwards of 30 years.[2] It comes as no surprise to learn that she was on 'extremely friendly terms' with Popes Pius IX and Leo XIII. Even into old age, her mental faculties remained largely unimpaired such that 'while the enterprises in which she was engaged were mainly religious and philanthropic, her interest in public, especially political, affairs never flagged, and her conversation remained, almost up to the end, remarkable for its preoccupation with large questions and events'.[3]

The end finally came on October 30th 1911. For all that some members of the family and the Anglican Establishment had excoriated her, the obituaries rightly acknowledged her remarkable achievements. The *Evening Mail* informed its readers that: 'For more than one religious institution she long collected several hundreds of pounds each year – not by annual subscriptions promised once for all, but by writing every succeeding year autograph letters to her many friends and acquaintances, and not desisting until the required sum was obtained. She heard

1   St Lawrence, 'Lady Elizabeth Herbert', pp. 41-42.
2   *Evening Mail*, 1 Nov. 1911.
3   *Evening Mail*, 4 Nov. 1911.

Mass at a very early hour; and her long day was one of ceaseless occupation … Probably no woman in modern days and certainly none in England, has done more for the church of Rome than Lady Herbert of Lea'.[1]

Lady Herbert was buried close to Vaughan at Mill Hill. But her contribution to Wilton was enormous. She was de facto chatelaine between 1846 and 1874; had Sidney lived another eight months she would have become Countess of Pembroke. In the event, two of her sons, George and Sidney, were to become 13th and 14th Earls. Only two previous women had been mother to two Earls, and none have been so since.

1   *Evening Mail*, 4 Nov. 1911.

FLORENCE NIGHTINGALE

LADY HERBERT'S INFLUENCE assisted the rise to prominence of two other women who had associations with Wilton. Best known of the two is Florence Nightingale. Florence was born in the city of that name on May 12th 1820. She was the second daughter of William and Frances Nightingale. Wealthy through inheritance, the Nightingales bought the Embley Park estate, near Romsey, in Hampshire in 1825. This brought them within twenty miles of the Herberts at Wilton. There is no evidence that the two families met before the late 1840s. The fact is not altogether surprising. However close geographically, the strongly Tory-Anglican Herberts were poles apart from the progressively Liberal and religiously Nonconformist (Unitarian) Nightingales.

It was the young Florence Nightingale's desire to break with social convention that would bring her into the orbit of the Herberts. As a teenager she became frustrated that her considerable intellect and drive were deemed best utilised by illuminating the drawing rooms of the idle rich. Florence became convinced that what she termed 'God's calling', pointed her to serving Him through the then less than respectable medium of nursing. Alarmed parents tried to stifle her wilfulness. One example of the latter was when Florence inveigled an invitation from Dr Richard Fowler, physician at the Salisbury Infirmary, to visit the institution in 1845. Her objective was to train as a nurse. But Dr Fowler was a friend of her parents; when all parties were fully apprised of what was afoot, Florence's scheme was vetoed. For the moment, therefore, she did not get to meet Sidney Herbert, chairman of the hospital's governing body.[1]

1 Bostridge, *Florence Nightingale*, ch. 4, esp. pp. 91, 93.

26. Florence Nightingale with Athena, her pet owlet, at Embley c. 1851.
From the sketch by her sister, Parthenope (Wikimedia Commons)

Florence first met Lizzie and Sidney Herbert two years later, in November 1847, 1,200 miles away in Rome. The Herberts were on their extended honeymoon tour; Florence was visiting the Holy City (it was hoped that a dose of foreign travel might cure her of the urge to nurse) under the watchful gaze of her parents' trusted friends, Charles and Selina Bracebridge. The encounter ranks as an important moment in history, marking as it does the start of a connection between Florence and Sidney ('a

time pregnant to me of all my future life' as Florence put it) which
would have profound consequences over the following decade. In
fact, it was the rapport established between Lizzie and Florence
in Rome which was the more obvious at the time, and which
ensured that the three would stay in touch. Despite the differences
between their respective families as outlined above, Florence and
Lizzie, only two years different in age, were strikingly similar:
privileged, bright, good looking and cultured; yet at the same
time religiously devout and wandering Europe (Florence would
describe herself as 'a vagabond' in a letter of 1850 much as Lizzie
did in her letter of 1848 to Manning) in search of ways to do
good.[1]

For a few weeks at the turn of 1847-8, however, Florence
and Lizzie were content to do their wandering in each other's
company during trips to galleries and on walking expeditions.[2]
On Christmas Eve Nightingale wrote to tell Dr Fowler, back
in Salisbury, that she had been watching Lawrence Macdonald
'an astute Scotchman, more practical than imaginative in his art
… doing Mr and Mrs Herbert's busts'. Since both can be seen
at Wilton today, the reader can judge for oneself whether 'Mr
Herbert's is remarkably good', but it was the real life Lizzie that
Florence had taken to describing as a 'sunbeam'.[3]

Florence remained in regular contact with the Herberts
on her return to England in April 1848. She received her first
invitation to visit Wilton almost immediately. It must be admitted
that she had little time for either the opulence of the house or its
treasures. She was content instead to run errands for Lizzie. More
formal employment of sorts came when Lizzie installed her briefly
as what we would now call a supply teacher in the School House
on the Wilton estate. She was also present at Wilton to act as
midwife to Lizzie on the birth of her third child, Elizabeth, on

1   Foster, *Sidney Herbert*, pp. 150-1.
2   Bostridge, *Florence Nightingale*, pp. 115-17.
3   McDonald, *Collected Works*, VII, pp. 139-47, 166-71, for Nighting-
gale to Fowler, 24 Dec. 1847, and Nightingale to her family, 12 Dec.
1847.

July 30th 1851.[1] When not at Wilton the Herberts were anxious
to consult their friend about the convalescent home they set up at
Charmouth in Dorset for persons working on the Wilton estate.
In 1851 they sought her advice on the appointment of a deaconess
to work there. In May 1854 Lizzie wrote to Florence for 'some
authentic information on the subject of the nurses [at St Bart's],
their bad pay and worse lodgings [in order that Herbert] could get
the evil more or less remedied, and public attention, at any rate,

27. The School House, Wilton Park (author's collection)

turned that way'.[2] And Lizzie had been between pregnancies when
she and Florence visited Mrs Tennant's Clewer House of Mercy
in March 1852.[3] Most crucially, however, once Mr Nightingale
was finally persuaded to grant Florence the annual allowance that
gave her the independence to pursue her ambitions, the Herberts
were amongst those who helped secure Florence's appointment

1   McDonald, *Collected Works*, VII, p. 771.
2   McDonald, *Collected Works*, XIII, p. 59, Mrs Herbert to Nightingale,
29 May 1854.
3   McDonald, *Collected Works*, VIII, p. 653.

as nursing superintendent in Harley Street in August 1853.
Florence was therefore only recognising the truth when, in notes
she compiled in 1857, she included the Herberts among those
of worth to her: 'They did not wait to send me to the Crimea in
order to support me, as far as they could, in doing God's work'.[1]

But send her to the Crimea they did. More precisely, Florence
and her nurses arrived at Scutari in Turkey. Here, converted army
barracks were serving as hospitals for those sick and wounded
transported the 800 miles from the battle zone across the Black
Sea. Conditions were every bit as bad as she had feared: the main
hospital was built over a sewer. There were already 3,000 patients;
battles at Balaclava and Inkerman, greatly compounded by
disease and the Russian winter, caused the number to escalate to
over 13,000 by February 1855. It was estimated that hospital beds
extended a distance of over four miles. Florence was immortalised
that month in a sketch showing her lamp in hand, wandering
the wards. But nursing, as she wrote to Sidney Herbert, 'is the
least of the functions into which I have been forced'. Male
chauvinism and distrust had meant that it was several days before
her party was even granted access to the hospitals proper. That
much achieved, Florence found herself spending money, some
of it her own, to buy the equipment, not least the basic straw
mattresses, so painfully lacking. She was thus more administrator
than nurse. Most of the latter were actually male orderlies but her
own coterie did not escape her beady eye. Two Presbyterians from
Edinburgh were sent home 'directly' following an alcohol-fuelled
Saturday night out with an orderly. Informing 'Dearest' Lizzie of
the episode, Florence lamented that 'under any guardianship less
watchful than mine, I can hardly depend on any Nurse'.[2]

Mercifully, Nightingale's initiatives and better weather
contributed to falling admissions and a lower death rate by the early
spring of 1855. This lessening of pressure allowed Florence to visit

---

1   McDonald, *Collected Works*, V, p. 236.
2   Goldie, *Letters*, p. 112, Nightingale to Mrs Herbert, 16 Apr. 1855.
For a general account of the debacle at Scutari see Bostridge, *Florence
Nightingale*, ch. 9.

the Crimea itself in May 1855. She fell almost fatally ill (modern medical experts incline to a diagnosis of chronic brucellosis) but refused to go home. She made two more inspection visits to the Crimea before the war ended in March 1856. Throughout the previous eighteen months, her friends and patrons from Wilton House had worked tirelessly on her behalf: Lizzie in helping to maintain a supply of nurses; Sidney from inside government chivvying and exhorting it to do more to assist her. More than that, the Herberts played an immeasurable role both in helping to sustain her morale and in acting as safety valves through which Florence could vent her frustrations.[1] It was this, perhaps, that Florence had in mind when she wrote to Lizzie early in 1858 that 'I always consider you and Mr Herbert are the authors of all the little good I have done in life'.[2]

Florence returned to England in August 1856. She was at the height of her fame. Yet, as is now generally forgotten, her most important work lay ahead. In this, her oft-repeated mantra was 'I stand at the altar of murdered men and whilst I live I fight their cause'. More than anybody she was only too aware that, of the 94,000 men sent to war, 4,000 had died of wounds and 19,000 more from disease. Although she does not appear to have visited Wilton ever again (illness meant that she rarely went anywhere) Florence's essential ally, freed from the trammels of office, in her war on preventable deaths amongst servicemen was Sidney Herbert. The two met for the first time in nearly two years in September. But it was Florence's terrier-like determination (she had no qualms in enlisting Queen Victoria and Prince Albert) which persuaded the government to accede to her demand for a royal commission into the sanitary sate of the army in May 1857.[3]

Three months of hard graft followed. Whilst Herbert, as MP and chair of the commission, was the public face of proceedings, Florence was assiduous in helping to select witnesses, prepare

---

1   Foster, *Sidney Herbert*, pp. 277-81.
2   McDonald, *Collected Works*, VIII, pp. 657-8, Nightingale to Mrs Herbert, 7 Jan. 1858.
3   Bostridge, *Florence Nightingale*, chs 11-12.

questions, and above all, in gathering and analysing data. Not for nothing was she elected the first female member of what became the Royal Statistical Society in 1858; her work at this time popularised the use of the pie chart. A grateful Herbert wrote to her as their labours drew to a close of 'how much I owe you for all your help during the last three months ... I should never be able to make you understand how helpless my ignorance would have been among the Medical Philistines. God bless you'. He had earlier had to employ all his fabled charm in dissuading Florence from appearing as a witness herself. Florence had to content herself with 35 pages of written responses. But she gave full vent to her frustration over shortcomings in the Crimea, and the more immediate problem that healthy young men died needlessly because they were quartered in insanitary barracks, in a private report some 830 pages long.[1]

The royal commission resulted in four sub-commissions being established, the most important of which required army barracks and hospitals to be put in sanitary order. Florence would feel vindication in the fact that the death rate of the army at home fell from 17 per thousand in 1855 to 9.95 per thousand in 1860. But she was less pleased – because it would necessarily divert his energies elsewhere – that Herbert agreed to re-join the government in April 1859 as Secretary for War. Worse, he was unwell, thereby thwarting her aspiration that she might work behind the scenes in helping him to reform the dinosaur commonly known as the War Office. But as it became clear that Herbert's illness might prove terminal, her concern switched to the personal: convinced that she knew better than the doctors, she offered exhaustive advice (chiefly that he rest) for his recovery. It availed nothing. Herbert died on August 2nd 1861. Lizzie recorded that amongst his final words were 'Poor Florence! Who will carry on our joint work?'[2]

Inclined to depression, and beset by debilitating ill-health, Florence believed that her useful life would end with Herbert's

---

1   Bostridge, *Florence Nightingale*, chs 12-13.
2   Foster, *Sidney Herbert*, chs 11-12.

death: 'God has taken from her the opportunity of giving my life's work'.[1] This proved untrue. Her main interest, already aroused when Sidney died, became India. She gathered and collated a huge amount of data for the sanitary commission on India which reported in 1863. And although she never visited 'the jewel in the crown', she came to be regarded as a leading oracle on ways in which its dazzle might be enhanced. Her initial concern, to nobody's surprise, was the condition of the barracks in which British troops were stationed. Over time she also became an advocate of schemes, for example improved irrigation and drainage and the need for a pure water supply, which would benefit the general population. It was said that no new Viceroy of India (there were fifteen between 1861 and her death) dared leave British shores before he had visited Miss Nightingale.[2]

Issues pertaining to medical care for the needy at home, however, were not neglected. Hospital design was something in which Florence took keen interest: the Salisbury Infirmary was one which turned to her for advice. She was patron of a pioneering project to train midwives and a vociferous supporter of the need to provide trained nurses in workhouse infirmaries, hitherto the feared destination of the sick poor. What became an embryonic system of district nursing received her endorsement too. In later years she took pride in the Nightingale Training School for Nurses which the Herberts had done so much to help establish. It was, as Benjamin Jowett, the celebrated Master of Balliol College, Oxford, told her in 1889, a remarkable curriculum vitae: 'you work on in silence, and nobody knows how many lives are saved by your nurses in hospitals (you have introduced a new era in nursing); how many thousand soldiers would have fallen victim to bad air, bad water, bad drainage and ventilation, are now living owing to your forethought and diligence; how many lives of India (they might be counted probably by hundreds of thousands) have

---

1   McDonald, *Collected Works*, I, pp. 327-8. Uncatalogued letter at Wilton House seen by kind permission of Lord Pembroke, Nightingale to Count Strzelecki, 18 Dec. 1861.
2   B.M. Dossey, *Florence Nightingale*, pp. 267-90, 355-74.

28. Wilton House from a woodcut of 1865 by W. Lydon
(author's collection)

been preserved by the energy of a sick lady who can scarcely rise
from her bed'. Belated recognition came in 1907 when she was
awarded the Order of Merit, the first woman to be so honoured.
When she died, in August 1910, the Crown made the offer of
a State Funeral in Westminster Abbey. It would have been the
first for a non-royal British woman. Her family, out of respect for
Florence's wish for an unfussy departure, laid her to rest in the
family vault in Hampshire.[1]

Florence would be reunited with Sidney Herbert in February
1915 when Arthur Walker's statue of her was set alongside that
of Herbert by John Foley. The latter had been outside the War
Office since 1867 but wiser heads decided that the two would
best be sited in front of the memorial to guardsmen who had died
in the Crimea, erected in Waterloo Place off Pall Mall, in 1861.
Though obviously appropriate in some ways, the decision was
also perplexing: Sydney Holland, who had acted as treasurer to
the committee commissioning Nightingale's statue, was on record
as saying that 'Herbert wished to marry Florence Nightingale'.[2] It

1   Dossey, *Florence Nightingale*, esp. ch. 15 and part 5.
2   Bostridge, *Florence Nightingale*, pp. 523-5.

was a popular perception which received its fullest endorsement in 1951 when Nightingale was memorably portrayed on screen by Anna Neagle in *The Lady with a Lamp*. As recently as 2018, a partially fact-based book, *A Divine Experience*, made much of the premise that Florence might have had a child by Sidney.

The truth is at once less sensational and more complex. Florence was initially in awe of the brilliant man she met in 1847. She became a friend but was always deferential to him (in a way that she was not when writing to Lizzie) during the Crimean period. In the later 1850s she was very close to him, claiming that he was 'a statesman [albeit no more] with whom I worked not daily, but hourly, for five years'. Only after Herbert's death did Florence came to treat him as a cynosure. Hours after his passing she wrote to Lady Herbert that 'No one ever loved him and served him as I did [...] After you, no one can mourn him as I do'. By 1865, in a private letter to a cousin, she was bemoaning 'How little his wife knows him'. Given now to calling Herbert 'her master' she became, unwittingly or otherwise, a rival to Lady Herbert as the keeper of Sidney's flame. One major reason why Arthur Stanmore took so long to complete his life of Herbert was because Florence refused to hand over – for more than a decade – documents relating to the seminal period of 1854-6.[1]

The coda to the relationship between Florence and Lady Herbert is at best ambivalent. 'Her visits always tear me to pieces', confided Florence in 1867. She condoled with Lady Herbert in September 1870 when her third son (Nightingale referred to him as *'my'* boy), sixteen year old William Reginald, perished at sea when HMS *Captain* sank with virtually all hands. Lady Herbert in turn sent Florence her condolences when her father died in 1874.[2] But the next letters to survive between the two were not written until 1890 when Lady Herbert solicited Nightingale's thoughts as to Roman Catholics being allowed to train as nurses at the Nightingale School. Florence's reference, in replying, that

---

1   Foster, *Sidney Herbert*, pp. 443-4, 451-3.
2   McDonald, *Collected Works*, VIII, pp. 696, 700-701.

'we can never misunderstand one another', rings distinctly hollow. Most of the correspondence between the two thereafter relates to the existence or non-existence of Sidney's letters. An exception, a fragment of a letter from the mid-1890s, sees Florence write that it was best for her not to see Lady Herbert when she was next in London. The woman who was for so long her 'dearest friend' was now described as 'Sidney Herbert's widow'.[1]

It was a sad ending to what could have been so very different. What if Lady Herbert had died in childbirth in 1861 and Sidney had recovered from Bright's disease to become Lord Pembroke in 1862? Had he chosen to remarry, Florence was far and away the obvious candidate. The scenario of Florence as Countess of Pembroke is not entirely unimaginable. As it was, the fates were content simply to introduce Florence to Sidney and Elizabeth Herbert. Without them, Miss Nightingale's story might never have taken flight.

1   McDonald, *Collected Works*, VIII, pp. 708-9.

SELINA BRACEBRIDGE

F EW TODAY REMEMBER Selina Mills. She was never especially feted in her lifetime, a fact which both Lizzie and Sidney Herbert found frustrating. For they, more than most, knew how important Selina was in the making of Florence Nightingale – the indispensable conduit which had thrown them together, and an important prop to Nightingale at the height of her fame.

Selina was born in 1800, the daughter of William Mills of Bisterne Park, Ringwood, twenty miles south of Wilton. In 1824 she married Charles Holte Bracebridge, of Atherstone Hall near Nuneaton, a man who liked to claim that he was descended from Lady Godiva. As a young couple, he and Selina were great travellers. They also immersed themselves in good works, notably as prominent members of the campaign which bought Shakespeare's birthplace in Stratford-upon-Avon in 1847.[1] Their less aesthetic causes included prison reform and education. They were, Florence Nightingale wrote, on account of their incessant charitable deeds, 'always starving themselves for somebody'.[2]

The Mills, Herbert and à Court families had long known each other in county politics and society but it was only the Liberal Mills's who became friendly with the similarly Liberal Nightingales before the 1840s. Selina thereby got to know the young Florence. It was she who prevailed upon Mr and Mrs Nightingale to let Florence accompany her and Charles on their trip to Rome in 1847. Friendly also with Lizzie Herbert, though it is by no means clear when and how, it was Selina who introduced the two in the Eternal City. In March 1848, by which time the Herberts had moved on to Sicily, Lizzie was dying to hear news of

---

1   McDonald, *Collected Works*, I, p. 523.
2   McDonald, *Collected Works*, I, p. 803.

'the dear Bracebridges'.[1]

Back in England, Selina was foremost, more so than the Herberts, in supporting Florence's desire for a life of service. She told Mrs Nightingale in 1850 that 'The opinion of the world has much changed … Young ladies in society … do things <u>now</u> of this kind … they are not in any way looked down upon because they devote themselves to Hospital or Patients'.[2] Sidney Herbert, mindful of the importance of their mutual friend when he invited Nightingale to head a nursing party to Scutari in 1854, told her that he was asking Selina too, since she could 'give you all the comfort you wd. require, and wh. her society & sympathy only could give you'.[3] In the week between invitation and departure Selina sat alongside Lizzie Herbert as one of the small team who interviewed the would-be nurses. Hers was a no-nonsense approach. She fired questions, staccato-like, and not infrequently delivered a brusque 'She won't do; send her out'.[4]

Selina shared a small room with Nightingale at Scutari. She would be her devoted factotum over the next nine months. Through her letters, the Herberts were provided with another set of eyes informing them of the realities of what was unfolding.[5] On at least one occasion Selina sat up alone into the early hours (even Florence had gone to bed) holding the hand of a dying soldier.[6] When Florence crossed the Bosphorus to the Crimea proper, in May 1855, it was Selina, the former reported, who 'keeps the bear-garden at Scutari'.[7] She and Charles finally left for England on July 28th 1855. Florence confided privately that 'For nine months she has been the moving power by which those hospitals were made to go at all – and no one can tell what she has been to me … almost my Holy Ghost'.[8] The subsequent allegation (by a

1   Bostridge, *Florence Nightingale*, pp. 115-17.
2   Bostridge, *Florence Nightingale*, pp. 130-41, 147.
3   Goldie, *Letters*, pp. 23-25.
4   Bostridge, *Florence Nightingale*, p. 209.
5   Bostridge, *Florence Nightingale*, pp. 250, 270.
6   Sir E.T. Cook, *Life of Florence Nightingale*, I, p. 236.
7   Goldie, *Letters*, pp. 126-7.
8   Goldie, *Letters*, p. 137.

29. Selina Bracebridge (Wikimedia Commons)

disgruntled nurse, and never substantiated) that Selina had been allowing nurses unfettered access to the Free Gift Shop was the only – and hardly heinous – blemish on her record of war service.[1]

The Herberts wanted to see Selina properly lauded. In pursuit of this end, Sidney presided at Selina's only public appearance in Wilton in October 1855. 'To that friend' he told the audience of 500 crammed into the town's library, 'he would tender his thanks on their common behalf'. The Reverend Sidney Godolphin Osborne, himself just returned from the war zone, elaborated: 'Mrs. Bracebridge … had nobly supported [Nightingale] in her labours. The work they had done … would have been too much for the endurance of an Englishman, but they were not too much for that of English women … Let them conceive what must have been the sufferings of the wounded when they amounted to thousands, and when those whose duty it was to attend to them were harassed as themselves. It was at such moment that these ladies stepped into the gap – restored order, and made these hospitals what they should have been. They infused hope by their presence where without it there had been despair. It was not without cause, therefore, that he said the future page of history would hand down these ladies as the best and noblest of their sex'.[2]

History, however, has chosen to distribute its favours unevenly. Selina took up new causes such as the reform of prisons for females, and 'the recreation and improvement of the artisans and working men', but she would never enjoy national celebrity.[3] When she died, at Upper Norwood in London on January 31st 1874, the newspapers took little notice.[4] It is by no means clear how frequently she visited Wilton as a friend of the Herberts, though it is known that she endeavoured to be either with

1   M. Vicinus and B. Nergaard (eds), *Ever yours, Florence Nightingale*, p. 129.
2   *SWJ*, 13 Oct. 1855.
3   *Leamington Spa Courier*, 20 July 1872.
4   *Leamington Spa Courier*, 20 July 1872, 7 Feb. 1874.

Lizzie or Florence on the anniversary of Sidney Herbert's death.[1] Nightingale wrote, on Selina's passing, that she 'was more than mother to me … And what would many have been without her … hers *was* faith, real sympathy with God … she lived to make others better: such real Christian humility … the most active heart and mind and buoyant soul that could well be conceived'.[2] The 'buoyant soul' gave some of her memorabilia from the Crimean War to Lady Herbert of Lea. It survives in glass cases, preserved at Wilton House to this day.

1   McDonald, *Collected Works*, VIII, 8, p. 693, Nightingale to Lady Herbert, 19 Sept. 1863.
2   McDonald, *Collected Works*, I, pp. 705-6.

Lady Gertrude Talbot

Six months after the death of Selina Bracebridge, Wilton welcomed its first resident Countess of Pembroke since 1827. Her husband, George Robert, eldest son of Sidney and Elizabeth Herbert, had been 13th Earl since the death of his Uncle Robert in April 1862. But since he was only eleven years old at the time he had not been in immediate need of a wife. His more pressing concern was better health, and knowledgeable doctors prescribed foreign travel as a remedy. Pembroke's account of some of them, *South Sea Bubbles,* which appeared in 1872, became something of a best seller. It relayed details of a voyage to the Pacific in 1870. In Tahiti he had met an ageing Queen Pomare IV, who furnished him with letters of introduction to her daughter-in-law, Princess Moe, of Taha. The Earl described her as 'a tall, graceful wonderfully pretty girl … She had rather a large but well-shaped head with an unusual amount of red forehead, under which were a pair of the biggest, roundest, shyest, gentlest, quietly laughingest (bother the adjectives!) eyes I have ever saw, a small retroussé nose, and a lovely little mouth that puckered her cheeks with cosy little dimples whenever she smiled; the ladylike gentleness of her manner, and the quaintness and naivete of her words and ideas were most charming'.[1] Her husband, 'Tomatoe', whose Anglicised name perhaps made it difficult for his English-speaking visitor to treat with due deference, was a volatile character. That volatility proved fatal shortly after Pembroke's departure. Learning of 'Tomatoe's' demise, and mindful that Moe was 'an interesting widow, with only one infantile encumbrance' the Earl 'deliberated whether I should go back and propose to her'. Further reflection convinced

1   13th Earl of Pembroke, *South Sea Bubbles*, p. 95.

him otherwise: 'my over-fastidious relations might object to the match. So I didn't'.[1]

Lady Herbert would surely have headed the list of 'over-fastidious relations'. But she could hardly object to her son's eventual choice of bride. A decade older than her husband,   Lady Gertrude Frances Talbot came from impeccable stock. She was the third daughter of the 18th Earl of Shrewsbury and Lady Mary Beresford, daughter of the 2nd Marquess of Waterford. It was the fourth marriage between a Herbert and a Talbot, albeit the first in over two centuries. The couple's mutually ancient pedigree was possibly why they were granted the unusual privilege of being married in King Henry VII's chapel in Westminster Abbey in August 1874. Lady Gertrude 'wore a dress of white satin antique, the skirt and train being draped with deep Brussels lace, basque body *en coeur*, puffed sleeves trimmed with lace ruffs, point de veil, with wreath of orange blossoms, and ornaments of diamonds and pearls'. The ceremony was followed by a wedding breakfast at the Talbots' home in Belgrave Square. Later that afternoon, Gertrude, the new Lady Pembroke, departed with her spouse, 'amid a shower of rice and satin slippers, for Wilton House … to pass the honeymoon, a special train on the South-Western Railway being engaged to take them to Wilton.'[2]

Neither Countess nor Earl was without eccentricities. 'The Pembrokes', it was remarked, 'were very advanced for the times in which they lived, for they both walked about the country without hats, so that many of their neighbours thought them quite mad'. Lady Pembroke especially 'always did what came into her head. She planted ivy all over the park, training it upon the trunks of the trees, and refusing to believe that anything so slender could possibly harm the forest trees which it so gracefully throttled … Her waywardness made her often alarming'. She would invite people to tea, forget, and then tell them to go away when they turned up. Perhaps the absence of headgear was not such a good idea after all?[3]

1   Pembroke, *South Sea Bubbles*, p.120.
2   *Wiltshire and Gloucestershire Standard*, 29 Aug. 1874.
3   Middelboe, *Edith Olivier*, p. 3.

30. Lady Gertrude Talbot by Sir William Blake Richmond, 1874

Personal idiosyncrasies aside, Lady Pembroke's reign as chatelaine offered a welcome period of stability after nearly a generation and more of uncertainty with respect to the title. Wilton would play host to 'most of the interesting people of the day'. Edward VII and Queen Alexandra visited in 1908, the occasion for the installation of a new-fangled technology known as bathroom plumbing. Gertrude's specific interests, however, appear to have lain beyond Wilton. Irish on her mother's side, she became interested in the training of nurses for workhouses in Ireland. 'The benefit of this to the poor in Ireland', it was judged, 'had been incalculable'.[1] Florence Nightingale would certainly have approved. Gertrude also established 'a large club for very poor boys in London for their recreation and education, which has had beneficial results in training them to be good and useful members of the State'. This probably alludes to the St Christopher's Working Boys' Club (they sent a wreath for her funeral), a youth club set up in Fitzroy Square in 1894. 'The housing of the working classes and the provision of good and innocent amusements for the poor were always subjects very near her heart'.[2] Wilton best remembers her today as the donor of the drinking trough and fountain which she presented to the town in 1901. It was given 'in memory of the happy times I spent amongst the Wilton people … I trust that the pure water will benefit the tired traveller and the weary horses and dogs'.[3]

Sadly, the 13th Earl's health never did improve: he died in May 1895, aged 44. He and Gertrude were childless. The Dowager Countess had presented a portrait of him to the borough not long before her own death on September 30th 1906.[4] She had been 'a great invalid ever since she became a widow'. Her funeral took place in Fugglestone Church in Wilton before her body was interred alongside that of the Earl. Most noticeable among the wreaths was a floral cross from Queen Alexandra (wife of Edward VII) bearing the inscription, 'In sorrowing remembrance of faithful friendship and old days'. It had, as the *Salisbury Times* wrote, been a dull day for a sad occasion.[5] But the tributes were warm, none more so than from the Reverend Dacres Olivier, at the end of his sermon in Wilton Church the following Sunday: 'She realised very distinctly the duties attaching to her station, and strove to befriend those about her with probably unusual consideration. Friendship towards those around is certainly not

1   *Salisbury Times*, 5 Oct. 1906.
2   https://aim25.com/cgi-bin/vcdf/detail?coll_id=4074&inst_id=13&nv1-browse&nv2=sub accessed 4 Feb. 2022.
3   *SWJ*, 3 Aug. 1901.
4   *The Times*, 1 Oct. 1906.
5   *Salisbury Times*, 5 Oct. 1906.

always shown by a person in high place by bounty and spending money ... the late Lady Pembroke was one prompt to accord such sympathy, if unable to give other help ... She was a warm-hearted, kind friend; friend to the neighbourhood, and this place; friend to very many individually, and friend, particularly by signifying without ostentation, her sympathy and her interest distinctly in what concerned her as resident in her historic home'.[1]

1   *Salisbury Times*, 12 Oct. 1906.

LADY BEATRIX LAMBTON

P ROMINENT AMONGST THE mourners at Gertrude, Dowager Countess of Pembroke's funeral was her brother-in-law Sidney, Lady Herbert's second son, who had succeeded as 14th Earl of Pembroke in 1895. He had served as MP for Wilton (1877-1885) and Croydon (1886-1895) before becoming Lord Steward of the Royal Household on his elevation to the peerage in 1895. His chief claim to distinction in the Lower House was to be regarded – though the competition may not have been stiff – as the handsomest of its 658 Members. His enthusiasm for sport was recognised when he became President of the Marylebone Cricket Club in 1896.

It was shortly after his first election as MP for Wilton that the future 14th Earl married Lady Beatrix Louisa Lambton, one of thirteen children of George Frederick Lambton, 2nd Earl of Durham and Lady Beatrix Hamilton, a daughter of the 1st Duke of Abercorn. The wedding took place at St George's Church in Hanover Square on August 29th 1877. Their relatively brief stewardship of Wilton ended with the Earl's death in 1913. During that largely uneventful period they are reported as having discharged the usual round of social engagements typical of their time and class. But Beatrix's 'consideration for the old people was witnessed in the home for four old natives of Wilton which she built there, and provided for'.[1]

Beatrix was destined to spend over 30 years as Dowager Countess. They began badly with an operation for appendicitis.[2] She was sufficiently recovered a few months later that, following the outbreak of the Great War, she was able to visit injured

1   *Western Gazette*, 24 Mar. 1944.
2   *Wiltshire Times*, 21 Mar. 1914.

31. Lady Beatrix Lambton with her sons Reginald, Lord Herbert, and The Hon George Herbert

servicemen on Salisbury Plain. She also crossed to Dublin to preside at a meeting of the linen guild whose members were making items for hospitals and the troops abroad.[1]

1   *Evening Irish Times,* 18 Nov. 1914.

Most of Beatrix's widowhood, however, was spent living with her younger, unmarried son, Colonel Sir George Herbert at Knoyle House in East Knoyle. Her name regularly appears in the local newspapers as having opened a fete or some other local event of that ilk. More unusual was her appearance in Mere, in May 1924, to speak at a meeting of the League of Nations Union.[1] Beatrix's two particular passions, though, were nursing and gardening. She was president of the East Knoyle, Sedgehill and Semley Nursing Association; and when the gardens at Knoyle House were open to the public during the summer months 'the Wiltshire Nursing Association benefited considerably'. She also oversaw a working party for St Nicholas' and St Martin's Orthopaedic Hospital at Pyrford in Woking.[2]

The Dowager Beatrix nearly died in 1940 after breaking a thigh during a fall in the garden at East Knoyle. But neither injury, old age (she was 80) nor war could yet silence her. She set up a group which met fortnightly at Knoyle House to make comforts for the men of the Wiltshire Regiment. But she also kept an eye on the next generation. As one tribute put it rather quaintly, she was 'concerned for the welfare of little children. She sought to make their young lives happy and so form their character when they were young and plastic'. At the close of 1943 she gave use of the upper floor of Knoyle House over to the Waifs and Strays Society (later known as the Church of England's Children's Society). Thus was born the Beatrix Nursery.[3] By then she had outlived her younger son (Sir George died in February 1942) but she was able to continue to live at Knoyle House because two of her grand-daughters, Phyllis and Guendolen Wilkinson, had come to live there. The latter was in charge of the nursery, having once worked as a nurse at Salisbury Infirmary.[4]

Following a short illness Beatrix died at Knoyle House on March 12th 1944. She was 84. At her request there were to be

1   *Western Chronicle*, 23 May 1924
2   *Western Gazette*, 17 Mar. 1944.
3   *Western Gazette*, 17, 24 Mar. 1944.
4   *Western Gazette*, 17 Mar. 1944.

*32. King Edward VII and party at the East Front side of Wilton House,
c. 1901*

neither mourning dress nor flowers; donations were invited instead
for the Beatrix Nursery. She was buried alongside her husband in
Wilton churchyard. A memorial service was held in East Knoyle
on March 22nd. In his address, the Right Reverend Dr Neville
Lovett, Bishop of Salisbury, extemporising on the themes of home
and beauty, rejoiced that Beatrix's life had provided him with
abundant material to work from: 'In her position she had the
choice of many spheres of influence, friendship and action. Her
choice lay where there was the greater need today, to the future
and for the sake of the next generation – the home. Beatrix, Lady
Pembroke, chose to use her gifts, her position and her personality
in loving kindness, neighbourliness, and to work amongst all
sorts and conditions of people where her home was, whether
at Wilton or at East Knoyle. She was a woman of great loving
kindness, consideration for others and a warm heartiness toward
her neighbours. Her concern was with the home – her own home
and the homes of others'.[1]

1   *Western Gazette*, 24 Mar. 1944.

SISTER MABEL MYRING

COUNTESSES OF PEMBROKE, and their illustrious female associates, clearly made more than a token contribution to nursing in the Victorian era. But they did not, as the Great War would, turn Wilton House into a hospital. Many stately homes joined it in opening their doors (to officers at least) in face of the overwhelming shortage of beds in military hospitals at home.

By 1915 there were at least a dozen hospital beds inside Wilton House, mostly in the private ground floor apartment created for the 10th Earl in the eighteenth century. Sadly, we do not know a great deal about what went on. A glimpse, at least, is provided by The Hon. David Herbert, socialite, writer, and second son of the 15th Earl and Countess. Amongst his earliest memories were

33. The water fountain in Wilton presented by Beatrix, Countess of Pembroke (author's collection)

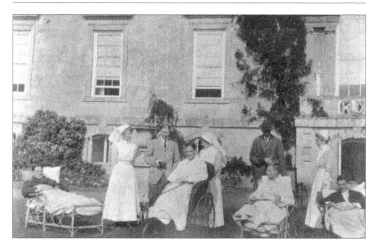

34. Wilton in the Great War c. 1916

'living in an improvised hospital in which my mother was always dressed in uniform as the Commandant, and hurried about the corridors and huge rooms, now bereft of all furniture except for the beds in the converted wards where the wounded lay. The house was filled with nurses, doctors and soldiers, some of whom were without arms and legs'. It was, he claimed, always noisy, with ambulances arriving all night long from Southampton.[1] Not all those who arrived would survive. Captain Terence Anthony Brabazon of the Essex Regiment, for example, was wounded in France on the eve of the Battle of the Somme in 1916. Having reached the sanctuary of Wilton, he sadly died in the house of septic pneumonia, in August that year. Aged just twenty, he is buried in Wilton cemetery.

There was, no doubt, a degree of exaggeration in the young David Herbert's account. Even so, official figures for December 31st 1918 record that 382 men had been admitted during the year, and that there had been a daily average of 50.6 patients occupying the 58 beds available. Although the war had ended on November 11th 1918, there were still 37 men occupying the 40 beds available on New Year's Eve that year. Total expenditure for

1   D. Herbert, *Second Son*, p. 16.

the year was £7,029 1s 9d. It was a far cry from the garden and shooting parties held in idyllic surroundings in the years before 1914.

The nursing at Wilton fell principally to four state registered nurses but they were assisted by a number (at least ten) of women from the Voluntary Aid Division (VADs). The latter, presumably drawn from the Wilton locality, would have undertaken basic nursing care and also have helped in the kitchen under the supervision of the estate's cook. The nurse about whom we currently know most is Sister Mabel Myring. Mabel, who began nursing in 1909, lived in Kensington Garden Square when she was registered as nurse 4992 in November 1915.[1] We do not know precisely when she came to Wilton, nor how long she stayed, but the words in the poetic tributes paid to her in an autograph book testify to the affectionate, often ironic, gratitude in which she was held by the men who encountered her. Consider the following composition, from June 1917, by a captain in the Royal Army Medical Corps:

> Who wakes me, I regret to say,
> At 8am & and every day,
> And drives my pleasant dreams away?
> It's Sister Myring
> 　Who reads my hand,
> fortells my fate,
> Says, "You are in a sorry state.
> Reform, my lad, before too late"?
> It's Sister Myring
> 　Then here's good luck to Sisters all,
> The dark, the fair, the short, the tall,
> The big, the small, the very small,
> And Sister Myring!

1　　https://kingscollections.org/nurses/m-o/myring-mabel-4992 accessed 5 Feb. 2022.

LADY BEATRICE PAGET

A NOTHER ENTRY IN Sister Mabel's autograph book, dated October 9th 1916, reads as follows.[1]

Life is mostly froth & bubble
Two things stand like stone
Kindness in another's Trouble
Courage in your own.

The writer was neither a patient nor a VAD but the 'Commandant', the designation afforded his mother by David Herbert. It was a peculiarly apt word for the formidable and eccentric lady who presided at Wilton throughout both World Wars.[2]

Beatrice Eleanor Paget was born on June 22nd 1883. Her father was Lord Alexander Paget, brother of the 4th Marquess of Anglesey, and a grandson of Henry William Paget. The latter (Lord Uxbridge and later 1st Marquess of Anglesey) had epitomised British sangfroid at Waterloo in 1815 by declaiming, 'By gad I've lost a leg', after losing said limb to a cannonball. Beatrice's mother, the Honourable Hester Alice Stapleton-Cotton, also boasted a distinguished military ancestry. She was the daughter of the 2nd Viscount Combermere, whose father, the 1st Viscount, Field Marshal Stapleton Cotton, had been one of the Duke of Wellington's most highly regarded subordinates

---

1   'B. Pembroke & Montgomery' was quoting lines from Adam Lindsay Gordon's *Ye Weary Traveller*. At the risk of incurring the late Commandant's wrath we would respectfully point out that 'trouble' should read 'struggle'. Lady Diana Spencer cited the lines at a fundraiser for breast cancer in Washington in 1996.
2   The following section draws heavily on David Herbert's memoirs of his mother as well as those of her friend Edith Olivier.

35. Beatrice, Countess of Pembroke, as 'Commandant nurse', 1918

during the Peninsular War. Such a pedigree suggested, rightly, that Beatrice was not a lady with whom to take liberties.

Lady Beatrice's upbringing, however, was not as gilt-edged as one might have supposed. Her father, Lord Paget, often absent from home, was selfish and parsimonious. The latter trait manifested itself in the small allowance he granted to his wife.

Hester, in an attempt to cut living costs, responded by taking Beatrice and her three siblings to live in Paris. Beatrice later said that said they were 'so badly off that until they were eleven or twelve they all wore sand-shoes, as leather shoes were too expensive'. Matters were only materially transformed when her eldest brother, 'Toppy', succeeded to the marquisate in 1898. For all his many perceived faults ('Toppy' was variously a spendthrift, a thief and a cross-dresser), at least some of his largesse (his 30,000 acres spread across several counties yielded £13,000,000 a year at current prices) was directed towards his mother and siblings.[1]

An awkward, perhaps ungainly child, Beatrice's mother was on record as finding her too bossy; she was known in the immediate family as 'long-legged Bee'. In appearance, at least, she blossomed as a teenager. A writer in the *Weekly Dispatch* in 1927 remembered how the tall and beautiful Bee Paget caught the eye at dance clubs.[2] Her admirers included Reginald, Lord Herbert. The couple were married at St Peter's, Eaton Square on January 21st 1904. The bride wore 'a dress of white crepe de chine embroidered in silk, in a design of lilies'.[3]

The Countess of Pembroke, as Beatrice became when her husband succeeded to the title as 15th Earl in March 1913, was soon featuring in the lifestyle magazine *Tatler*.[4] A year later, the Great War demonstrated to a wider public that she was no mere ornament. As early as September 1914, she wrote to the national press from Wilton to protest on behalf of women who had been 'making shirts, socks, sleeping helmets, comforters etc., for our soldiers at the front' only to be told that they were no longer needed. 'It will be disappointing', she concluded, 'to those who have so generously helped by giving money, and to those who have so generously helped by giving their services, in so many cases free of remuneration … to be told that the "Forwarding Officer at Southampton cannot accept any packages of clothing

1   D. Herbert, *Engaging Eccentrics*, pp. 49-51.
2   *Weekly Dispatch*, 9 Jan. 1927.
3   *Sheffield Daily Telegraph*, 22 Jan. 1904; *Tatler*, 27 Jan. 1904.
4   *Tatler*, 16 Apr. 1913.

which are outside the limits of the Post."'[1] As the war turned into one of attrition, she was to be found supporting a sale in Wilton to raise funds for the Red Cross, and at Mount Merrion, the Herbert's home in Ireland, to attend a hospital meeting. Given the Herbert family connection and her own involvement in nursing, it was entirely appropriate that she was in London to witness the unveiling of Florence Nightingale's statue alongside that of Sidney Herbert in February 1916.[2]

Beatrice's chief war work, however, was twofold. First, as noted earlier, she oversaw the improvised hospital for wounded officers in Wilton House. Refusing to be distracted by her 'many military admirers including generals of the Great War', she worked 'untiringly'. *The Bystander* published a photograph of the graceful and contemplative Countess in nurse's uniform in April 1918.[3] Beyond Wilton's walls, Beatrice responded positively to the suggestion made by her friend, Edith Olivier, that she should join those looking to do something 'to organise the employment of women on the land.' When Wiltshire's War Agricultural Committee was established, in November 1915, Beatrice was invited to join it; in February 1916 she was appointed chair of its hybrid Women's War Agricultural Committee. Anybody who doubted that she had done 'a marvellous job' was welcome to attend the regular committee meetings held in Trowbridge.[4] Formal recognition of her efforts came when she was awarded a C.B.E. in 1919.

What the wider public did not know was that Beatrice also had to play an increasingly active part in the affairs of the Wilton estate. Her husband was often called away by military duties. It was Lord Pembroke, for example, who was chosen (after all, he

1   *Evening Mail*, 18 Sept. 1914.
2   *Wiltshire Times*, 5 Feb. 1916; *Truth*, 18 Nov. 1916; *Dundee Courier*, 15 Feb. 1916.
3   Herbert, *Engaging Eccentrics*, p. 51; *The Bystander*, 10 Apr. 1918.
4   K. Luck, 'The growing pains of the "Women on the Land movement" in Wiltshire 1914-1917', *The Local Historian*, XLVII (2017), pp. 197-200; Olivier Papers 982/47, diary entry for 22 July 1915; *Wiltshire Times*, 30 Jan. 1954.

was a great-grandson of Catherine Woronzow) to present a field marshal's baton to Czar Nicholas II from George V in Petrograd in March 1916.[1] Such engagements diverted him from Wilton at a time when the estate was coming under financial strain. Death duties, first introduced in 1894, had fallen on the family twice in twenty years with the deaths of the 13th and 14th Earls in 1895 and 1913. In addressing the problem of paying them, it was the unsentimental Countess who took the lead. The first initiative was a much publicised sale of a portion of the family's library at Sotheby's in June 1914. Some 211 volumes were auctioned over two days, 'practically all dating from the fifteenth century', for £38,936.[2] In 1917, several paintings, 223 drawings, eight 'superb studies' by Albrecht Durer, and suits of armour acquired as war trophies by the 1st Earl, followed them out of the doors of the ancestral home. More prosaically, some of the family's Irish property was sold too.[3]

The coming of peace granted only temporary respite. The 15th Earl, for all that he had spent over twenty years in the army, was intelligent, amiable and kind. But he was also weak-willed. From the early 1920s, he embarked on a four year long love affair with Lois Sturt, twenty years his junior, the brightest of the bright young things of the 1920s. The Earl was eventually replaced in her affections by the Duke of Kent, but not before some of Lois's less circumspect friends had induced him to join them in a series of ill-judged investments. Bankruptcy notices were being issued against him in 1926: family members reckoned that his debts were £500,000.[4] In face of the revelations Beatrice told her children that 'You must face up to it like the rest of us and behave as if nothing has happened'.[5] Her errant husband, meanwhile, was summoned back to Wilton (in which he had shown even less interest since meeting Lois), and dutifully assisted whilst

1   *Western Times*, 2 Mar. 1916.
2   *Birmingham Daily Post*, 27 June 1914.
3   *Truth*, 13 June 1917.
4   *Western Gazette*, 2 July 1926; Herbert, *Second Son*, p. 29.
5   Herbert, *Second Son*, p. 29.

she made arrangements to pay off the creditors. Part payment, it may be presumed, was made possible by selling the fourteenth century Wilton diptych, the oldest and greatest of the family's art treasures, to the National Gallery in 1929.[1]

But there was a personal price to pay. Although the contrite Earl was reconciled, never to stray again, Beatrice was perceived by her children to have changed, at least to a degree. She became 'intensely nervous and reserved ... To us she became inhuman; simply "the boss."' In face of her formidable presence the Earl was reduced to a cypher.[2] Edith Olivier described the Countess in 1926 as follows: 'She cares for few people ... She is a strange woman with her pale pointed face, very dark eyes, eyebrows like accents circumflex, white hair – really rather Mephistophelian – hating all modern books and *most* people – talking very well and with great individuality – describing people most vividly in a few (generally very cruel!) words'.[3]

To the uninformed, outwardly at least, Wilton regained some of its pre-war glamour during the 1920s. Edward, Prince of Wales, was guest of honour at a ball in 1922.[4] Another grand ball was staged for Sidney, Lord Herbert's, coming of age in 1927: Edith Olivier described it as 'Unforgettable in its magic and majesty ... Lady P herself very striking and slim'.[5] A triumvirate of such glittering occasions was completed by a visit from the Queen of Spain in 1928.[6] And privately, as the years of greatest travail faded into recent memory, Beatrice could exhibit a lighter side to her character. In 1929, for example, she agreed to take part in a short film devised by her son, David Herbert, and his friends. She played a Russian spy who, having kidnapped a lady from the house, drove off with her through the streets of Wilton.[7] During

1   Herbert, *Second Son*, p. 150.
2   Herbert, *Second Son*, pp. 148-51.
3   Middelboe, *Edith Olivier*, p. 15.
4   *Belfast Telegraph*, 26 Oct. 1922.
5   Middelboe, *Edith Olivier*, pp. 52-53.
6   *Wiltshire Times*, 3 Nov. 1928.
7   Middelboe, *Edith Olivier*, pp. 88-89.

*36. Beatrice, Countess of Pembroke, and the 15th Earl in the Italian
Garden in their coronation robes, 1937*

the festive jollities of 1935, which centred on an improvised ballet
about Good King Wenceslas, she even consented to play the part
of the great St Edith. Equally congenial during the 1930s, she
formed part of a 'committee of taste' which, spearheaded by the
genius of Rex Whistler, redesigned the library on the west side of
the house.[1]

    Although Beatrice had persuaded a hundred students to part
with five shillings each for 'a summer school of Conservatism' at
Wilton in 1923, it was during the 1930s that she assumed a more

1   Middelboe, *Edith Olivier*, pp. 173-4; Robinson, *Wilton House*, pp.
233-5.

active role in the game of politics.[1] She made her formal entry
into local government in 1932 when she was returned (nobody
had dared oppose her!) as a county councillor for Wiltshire. The
following year she played host to the Prime Minister, Stanley
Baldwin and his wife, at Wilton.[2] A more familiar face at Wilton
during those years was Winston Churchill. Owing to his propensity
to descend around Whitsuntide, Beatrice took to calling such
occasions 'Winstontide'. Then in the process of enduring what he
called his wilderness years, Churchill found release in indulging
his passion for painting at Wilton. His subjects included the
antique statuary in the Upper Cloisters and, inevitably, the
picturesque Palladian Bridge.[3] Like Churchill, her new found
friend, Beatrice did not shy away from controversy. Her name
appeared in the newspapers at the end of 1938 when she asserted
that the Duchess of Windsor (following Edward VIII's abdication
in 1936 in order to marry the twice divorced American, Wallis
Simpson, the two had become Duke and Duchess of Windsor)
was not entitled to a curtsey. 'How … she is able to reconcile her
respect for the technicalities of etiquette with the courtesy she
owes as a great lady', thundered the *Weekly Dispatch*, 'is a matter
for Lady Pembroke's social conscience'.[4] Quite easily, one might
suppose.

World War II would bring both Churchill and Beatrice back to
front line action. In some respects, at least, it was an exciting time.
George VI paid a secret visit to Wilton only days after hostilities
commenced in September 1939.[5] Gossip had it, by December
1939, that Beatrice had fallen in love with the photographer Cecil
Beaton, a familiar face at Wilton (she was 56, he was 35), and that
she looked twenty years younger in consequence.[6] Beaton took
the opportunity whilst at Wilton that Christmas to co-author a

1 Middelboe, *Edith Olivier*, pp. 93-94.
2 *Wiltshire Times*, 30 Apr. 1932, 22 July 1933.
3 Herbert, *Engaging Eccentrics*, p. 74.
4 *Weekly Dispatch*, 18 Dec. 1938.
5 Middelboe, *Edith Olivier*, p. 217.
6 Middelboe, *Edith Olivier*, p. 218.

pantomime, *Heil Cinderella*, to raise money for the *Daily Sketch* War Relief Fund. Lady Pembroke consented to be president of the hastily convened ensemble, mostly consisting of friends and family. The run lasted only three nights (at Wilton anyway) from January 2nd 1940 before she resigned in disgust at the lack of sobriety and excessive adlibbing evident amongst some members of the company.[1]

The war became more serious during 1940. In June Wilton was commandeered to be the Headquarters of Southern Command. Those who visited were a veritable roll call of luminaries on the Allied side. They included King George VI, Churchill, and Generals Eisenhower, Alexander, Auchinleck and Montgomery. Beatrice and the Earl were confined to just three rooms of the house: they seem to have been less concerned that family treasures were moved aside (and even outside) than proud that Wilton was now 'a key military centre'.[2] But there were limits. As David Herbert recalled: 'My mother ruled Southern Command with a rod of iron. She insisted on a weekly inspection to see that there was no damage being done to the house. It might have been the Supreme Commander of the Allied Forces who was paying a visit, not just Lady Pembroke, mistress of the house. Generals, colonels, majors, captains were all as nervous as kittens on my mother's arrival each Monday morning. She was quite right, as certainly the damage would have been double if she had not insisted on these inspections'. Amongst the rank and file there were two areas for complaint that particularly irked her. She 'was permanently at war with military females' who saw no wrong in picking the flowers, including daffodils, jonquils and narcissi, which she had planted lovingly during the inter-war years. Male shortcomings manifested themselves in the graffiti scrawled on the eighteenth century temple designed by Sir William Chambers and situated on the rise above the Park. She marched the hapless commandant to inspect it; he conspired to aggravate her ill

1   Middelboe, *Edith Olivier*, pp. 222-3.
2   Middelboe, *Edith Olivier*, p. 233.

humour by suggesting that storm damage was perhaps to blame. 'My mother', wrote David Herbert, 'drew herself up to her full height and said, "Perhaps, Colonel, you are more fortunate than I am, in that you have witnessed gales carving initials into eighteenth century stone columns. Have your men up here by two o'clock, erase the initials, and tidy up the place generally and do not let this sort of thing occur again."' Presumably they tried, but some of the graffiti, now part of Wilton's history, remains there to this day.[1]

Beyond Wilton's gates Beatrice volunteered to be an air raid warden. In 1942 she was elected only the second female mayor in Wilton's history, and was then re-elected every year until 1946. At the start of 1943 *The Sketch* published a Cecil Beaton photograph of her in mayoral robes. Apparently she was finding time to delve into the borough records with a view to proving that Wilton was the oldest borough in England. 'Lady Pembroke', the editorial concluded, 'is by no means, a mere platform figure, for she helped at the local post-office to cope with the recent Christmas rush'.[2] The same year she was also prominent as organiser of the Wiltshire Rural Pennies section of the Red Cross Agriculture Fund. Over £20,000 was raised.[3]

Vestiges of Southern Command remained at Wilton until the later 1940s. Thereafter, as was the experience in many stately homes in the post-war period, lifestyles became somewhat 'diminished'. Fewer grand balls, and the closing up of rooms which were rarely used, helped to save money. In a further attempt to make ends meet, Beatrice, more out of pragmatism than enthusiasm (before the war she ordered David to charge friends of his, to whom she took a dislike, for tours of the house!), was persuaded to open Wilton to the public. Once the plunge was taken, 'The Countess threw herself wholeheartedly into the preparations. She helped recruit guides and impart the history of the house, grounds, family, picture and sculpture collections and

1   Herbert, *Engaging Eccentrics*, pp. 51-52.
2   *The Sketch*, 27 Jan. 1943.
3   *Wiltshire Times*, 17 July 1943.

furniture. She opened a restaurant in the stables and was even known to serve herself'. Wilton House and Grounds opened in 1951 with entry priced at half a crown. When the fancy took her Beatrice was even reputed to sit at the north-east corner of the Upper Cloisters and offer visitors a view of some of the private rooms for an extra sixpence.[1] The decision to throw open Wilton's doors to the public presumably explains the timing of a feature on Wilton (she appeared with dogs Bannock and Bumble), in *Tatler* on the eve of the second season.[2]

Beatrice and the Earl occasionally conducted guided tours themselves. One couple thus favoured (presumably non-paying) was the Queen and Prince Philip in February 1953. Popular lore has it that the fine white and gold china 250 piece dinner service presented to the 11th Earl in 1807, which was used during the visit, was later hand washed by the Countess herself. Perhaps it was whilst she was doing so that thieves ransacked her bedroom and made off with furs and jewellery worth £6,000.[3]

Life at Wilton House would never again be quite as sensational. Beatrice continued through the 1950s as chair of the Salisbury Infirmary, councillor (she served another term as mayor of Wilton in 1954), and magistrate. When the Earl died in 1960, she declined to move into Bulbridge House (the traditional abode of the Dowager Countess) in the town, preferring instead a flat in London. Her official departure after nearly half a century 'in post' (the longest of any Countess) was one of the rare recorded occasions when she shed a tear.[4] Her equanimity quickly restored, it proved difficult to find domestics who would tolerate her punctilio. The best was a septuagenarian former soldier who treated her with the same robustness John Brown was said to have displayed towards Queen Victoria. 'The trouble with you', he told

---

1   Herbert, *Engaging Eccentrics*, pp. 92-3; *Dundee Courier*, 25 Feb. 1953.
2   *Tatler*, 30 Apr. 1952.
3   *Dundee Courier*, 25 Feb. 1953.
4   Herbert, *Second Son*, pp. 152-3

her on one occasion, 'is that you are just a tough old countess'.[1] 'In truth', as David Herbert expanded, 'my mother resembled an eighteenth-century aristocrat. I am sure she would have been the first to go to the guillotine, and would have gone with great dignity and courage, pitying the poor wretches who were about to behead her'. 'Towards the end of her life', he added, 'she mellowed, but only up to a point. She could still be imperious and stubborn, having been accustomed to living in style and controlling Wilton and all its dependants'.[2]

Even in her late eighties, Beatrice treated her second son as if he were still a boy. Her grandchildren, by contrast, were indulged: she went gambling with them once a week. The wider family took to calling her (though whether to her face is unclear) 'Auntie Beeswax'. At home in London she liked to play canasta into the small hours.[3] It was here that she died, following a short illness, on February 8th 1973, aged 89. There was, inevitably, a final twist. Following cremation at Golders Green, Beatrice's ashes were taken to David at her London flat. Presuming that the package had been intended for his deceased mother, David begged to inform the delivery man that it had arrived too late. 'I am afraid, sir', the man replied, 'this *is* Lady Pembroke'. The ashes were taken down to Wilton to be interred in the new family burial ground on the estate – another of her ideas – without further incident.[4] The press paid very little attention to her passing but David Herbert surely reflected the opinion of many locals when he wrote that 'She had been respected and admired for all the public work she had done; and although she frightened some people with her directness, one and all admitted her sense of justice and dedication to whatever job she took on, and the efficiency with which she tackled any problem put before her'.[5]

1   Herbert, *Engaging Eccentrics*, pp. 46-47.
2   Herbert, *Engaging Eccentrics*, p. 173
3   Herbert, *Second Son*, p. 151.
4   Herbert, *Engaging Eccentrics*, pp. 47-49.
5   Herbert, *Engaging Eccentrics*, p. 48.

EDITH OLIVIER

WILTON WAS HOME to another extraordinary lady during the first half of the twentieth century. The Bishop of Salisbury told her in 1941, not entirely in jest, that she had 'put it back on the map!'[1] Her name, serendipitously, was Edith.

Edith Olivier was descended from early eighteenth century Huguenot stock.[2] Her family established itself in Wiltshire county society, notably around Chippenham, during the nineteenth century. They came to Wilton in the person of her father, the Reverend Dacres Olivier, when he was appointed curate in 1860. The Pembroke family, in whose gift it lay, made him Rector in 1867. The 14th Earl appointed him his personal chaplain in 1895. The Reverend Dacres finally retired, after 52 years' service, in 1912 and went to live in Salisbury's Cathedral Close where he died in January 1919.[3]

The eighth of her father's ten children, Edith was born in Wilton Rectory on December 31st 1872. As a young girl she was a welcome guest at Wilton House where she mixed with the nieces and nephews of the childless 13th Earl and Countess. It bred in her a social self-confidence which would prove invaluable. After a period of private tutoring she won a scholarship to read History at St Hugh's College Oxford in 1895. Her studies there would last only four terms before illness, induced by asthma, forced her to leave. But she was there long enough to become acquainted with her father's old friend, the Reverend Charles Lutwidge Dodgson, better known as Lewis

1   Middelboe, *Edith Olivier*, p. 245.
2   French Protestants who fled France for fear of prosecution after 1685 when Louis XIV revoked the Edict of Nantes which had granted them religious liberties.
3   *Wiltshire Times*, 11 Jan. 1919.

Carroll, author of *Alice's Adventures in Wonderland* (1865).[1] Had Edith stayed longer at Oxford she would not have graduated: although the University admitted women, it did not allow them to take degrees until 1920.

Edith's life over the next twenty years fell something short of wonderland. When her mother, Emma Eden, died in 1908, she and her sister Mildred took over the running of the rectory in Wilton. They moved with their father, a martinet where the running of the household was concerned, when he retired to Salisbury. Edith was at least allowed enough free time to expand the number of her social contacts and thereby gain a taste for activism. She became a member of the Primrose League, whose aim was to spread Conservative principles; the Imperial League, whose aim was to foster the unity of the Empire, and the League for Opposing Women's Suffrage.[2] Lest anybody be in any doubt, Edith's politics were right of centre.

It was the issue of employing women to ease labour shortages during the Great War, however, that brought Edith to greater prominence and allowed her to demonstrate her capacity for organisation. With the support and blessing of Lady Pembroke, who was its chairperson, Edith was appointed secretary for South Wiltshire when the Wiltshire Women's War Agriculture Committee was set up in February 1916. Her chief tasks included compiling a register of female volunteers, and helping to dispel the doubts exhibited by farmers that those on it would be of much use. Towards the first objective there was measurable progress. Before war broke out, 1,077 women were being employed on 290 farms; by October 1916 Edith was able to report that there were 3,154 names on the register and that 2,655 women were being employed by 1,038 farmers.[3] On the second point, however, that of confronting male prejudice, progress was less encouraging. Never afraid to enter the lion's den, Edith's diary for December 29th 1916 records that she went to a farmers' meeting to 'make

1   Middelboe, *Edith Olivier*, pp. 3-8.
2   Luck, 'The growing pains', p. 197.
3   *Wiltshire Times*, 21 Oct. 1916.

37. Edith Olivier c. 1937 (Wikimedia Commons)

'em say what they thought women could do. I heard them whisper "scare-crows" to each other'.[1]

Edith did not deny that the aptitude of the volunteers was variable. In private she referred dismissively to two young

1   Luck, 'The growing pains', p. 202; Olivier Papers 982/47, diary entry for 29 Feb. 1916.

women from Bournemouth as 'stinking of piers and parades.'
Finding those capable of milking cows was, she admitted in
public, especially vexing.[1] But Edith persisted. She became
superintendent of the Wiltshire branch of the Women's Land
Army after it was founded in 1917. In 1919, when it was
disbanded, Edith, 'our beloved country organising secretary, "a
real sport" and friend of the girls', handed out badges to those
who had served.[2] Her own services were acknowledged when
she was awarded an M.B.E. in 1920.

The early 1920s would prove pivotal in Edith's life thanks to
a more worldly 'award'. The 15th Earl invited Edith and Mildred
to move into the Daye House (originally a milk parlour) on the
edge of Wilton Park beside the Netherhampton road. Had fate
not decreed otherwise, the sisters might then have been content
to live out their remaining decades in relative anonymity. But
Mildred, aged just 51, died from breast cancer in November
1924. Plunged into depression, Edith equivocated over entering
an Anglian Convent. The Mother Superior rightly scotched the
idea: Edith was 'too rebellious of mind for a life of prayer and
contemplation'. Instead, she accepted an invitation to visit San
Remo in Italy. Here, in March 1925, she met a young art student
(she was 52, he was 19) called Rex Whistler. Their friendship,
which blossomed more or less overnight, was the most important
of her life.

'Suddenly', wrote Cecil Beaton of the Edith who returned
to England, 'the country robin emerged as a bird of paradise'.[3]
Beaton's image came alive when Whistler persuaded her to acquire
a less conventional wardrobe and a more fashionable ('bob')
hairstyle. For the rest of Edith's life the Daye House became,
as Beaton remembered it, home to 'a strange heterogeneous
company – actors, bishops, archaeologists and professors'.[4]

1   *Wiltshire Times*, 12 Feb. 1916; Olivier Papers 982/47, diary entry
for 12 Aug. 1916.
2   *Wiltshire Times*, 6 Sept. 1919.
3   C. Beaton, *The Wandering Years. Diaries: 1922-1939*, p. 164.
4   C. Beaton, *The Years Between. Diaries: 1939-44*, p. 16.

Beaton was right but it was the cast of figures drawn from the arts and literature that stand out. The poet Sir Henry Newbolt (1862-1938), lived at Netherhampton, only a few hundred yards away. Writers who descended on the Daye House included Osbert (1892-1969) and Edith Sitwell (1887-1964). Siegfried Sassoon (1886-1967), poet and writer, lived at Teffont Magna, seven miles west of Wilton; later, at Heytesbury, childhood home of Lady Herbert of Lea. Prominent amongst the artists of Edith's acquaintance were the Australian, Henry Lamb (1883-1960), and Augustus John (1878-1961), who had a home near Fordingbridge. However, it was the coterie of younger aesthetes – Edith defined them as 'a group of young men who carry lilies down the street and wear wondrous womenish clothes ... with brains and character (even if not too moral)' – who were drawn to the Daye House as if to a magnet. They included the poet John Betjeman (1906-1984), '*cleaner* than I expected... loves Georgian churches'; and the composer, William Walton (1902-1983). The latter, 'a very domestic man', wrote part of his first symphony (premiered in 1934) at the Daye House. Lord David Cecil (1902-1986), biographer and scholar, whom Edith thought 'A most captivating creature', lived at Rockbourne, ten miles south of Wilton. Defying categorisation, but 'dazzling in his inspired wit and vision', Stephen Tennant (1906-1987), who lived at Wilsford Manor seven miles north of Wilton, is remembered now chiefly for his decadent lifestyle. A more frequent visitor than any of them was Cecil Beaton (1904-1980) photographer of society and fashion, who 'enjoys congenial society and indeed any society for he loves being able to criticise'.[1] Edith helped him find Ashcombe House in Berwick St James, near Salisbury, which he leased for fifteen years from 1930.

But not even Beaton could eclipse Rex Whistler (1905-1944). It has been written that Edith transformed him socially and intellectually from 1925 just as he had transformed her outward appearance in 1925. Whistler delighted in Wilton and Edith, as

1   Middelboe, *Edith Olivier*, pp. 75, 98, 139.

his many surviving representations of both can testify. She once described him as 'the reincarnation of Breughel'. Their friendship was facilitated when Rex and his brother Laurence (1912-2000), best known for his glass engraving, took a lease on the Walton Canonry in Salisbury Cathedral Close during the 1930s. It was presumably through Edith and Beatrice, Countess of Pembroke, that Whistler received one of his best remembered commissions: *Capriccio* is the title of the giant mural that adorns the dining room at Plas Newydd, seat of Beatrice's brother, the Marquess of Anglesey. Rex was intending to return to Plas Newydd when

38. The Daye House (author's collection)

his war service with the Welsh Guards ended. But he was killed by a shell in Normandy on July 18th 1944. Edith never really recovered from the blow; Rex was both the son and husband she never had.[1]

It is impossible to resist comparing Edith's entourage at the Daye House with the Wilton of Mary Sidney – and Aubrey's

1   A. Thomasson, *A Curious Friendship*, pp. 457-8.

remark that she was 'the greatest patroness of wit and learning of any lady in her time'. Mindful of it herself, Edith sometimes saw Rex Whistler in the guise of Sir Philip Sidney. The comparison is not, of course, absolute. In Mary Sidney's time Wilton was a draw more for the established than the rising literati. And whilst Mary Sidney brought luminaries to Wilton to perform, Edith provided her emerging talents with encouragement within the sanctuary of the Daye House. She was less a patron than sounding board. As Beaton put it, 'So many of the young writers, painters and poets came to her with problems about their work and their lives and they knew that after she had listened intently to their outpourings, her advice would be unprejudiced, wise and Christian'.[1]

Something of the world Edith inhabited at Wilton and its environs was captured by Beaton in his atmospheric black and white photographs: some of them are exhibited at Wilton to this day. It is only fair to point out, however, that not everybody approved of the hedonism portrayed in his flamboyant images. Beaton was shocked that when Stephen Tennant appeared in Wilton for the parade to mark George V's Silver Jubilee, in 1935, he was received with a 'barrage of rude remarks showered on him by total strangers'.[2] But this was, after all, the 'hungry thirties'. Beaton, more than most, should have known better. In 1927 he had been amongst the party which accompanied Edith to the Ball in honour of Sidney, Lord Herbert's, coming of age. Tall and willowy in appearance, with long hair, and a delicate walk, Beaton proved an irresistible lure to several of the more traditional bloods present. Beaton wrote that 'The black night whirled past me, batlike, as the phantasmagoria journey continued, until abruptly, with a vicious thrust from all my attackers, I was catapulted into the Nadder'. Or, to put it in language which ordinary Wiltonians might have used, he was thrown into the river near the Palladian Bridge. 'Do you think the Bugger's drowned?' revealed at least a vestige of concern on the part of one of his assailants.[3] Beatrice,

1   Middelboe, *Edith Olivier*, p. 302.
2   H. Vickers, *Cecil Beaton*, p. 183.
3   Beaton, *The Wandering Years. Diaries: 1922-1939*, pp. 171-2.

who was indulgent of Edith's set, was furious when told what had happened: 'Mr Beaton was just as much a guest in her house as they were, and would they please leave immediately'.[1]

The parties, play-acting, and pageantry in which Edith and her friends indulged were, for her, in part a hankering after a lost dream to be an actress,[2] Laurence Olivier, who was at the height of his fame during the Second World War, and who met Edith at Wilton, was a distant cousin. But she had discovered, and would discover, other arenas in which she could perform. By the time she met her namesake, Edith had established herself as an author in the tradition (though not the style!) of Mary Sidney and Lady Herbert of Lea. An early, if ephemeral, example of her work was *Blue Beaver*, a pantomime performed in 1923 in the Old Riding School at Wilton and elsewhere in aid of local hospital and nursing charities.[3] A handful of novels followed: *The Love Child* (1927), *As Far As Jane's Grandmother's* (1928), *The Triumphant Footman* (1930), *Dwarf's Blood* (1930) and *The Seraphim Room* (1932). Edith's non-fiction titles included *The Eccentric Life of Alexander Cruden* (1934), *Mary Magdalene* (1934), *Country Moods and Tenses* (1941), and *Four Victorian Ladies of Wiltshire* (1945). There were two autobiographical volumes: one was the thinly disguised *Night Thoughts of a Country Landlady - Being the Pacific Experiences of Miss Emma Nightingale in Time of War* (1945); the other, more successful, was *Without Knowing Mr Walkley* (1938). This detailed the characters of her youth and her work during the Great War. It also revealed a fascination (some say eccentricity) for the supernatural. This apparently dated to 1916 when Edith stopped at Avebury to watch a village fair that was in progress: only later did she discover that the last one held there had taken place well over half a century previously. For the modern reader seeking to enter Edith's mind and world, however, there is nothing to rival the published extracts from her voluminous journals.

1   Vickers, *Cecil Beaton*, pp. 98-9; Herbert, *Second Son*, pp. 44-45.
2   Middelboe, *Edith Olivier*, p. 2.
3   *Wiltshire Times*, 27 Jan. 1923.

History was Edith's favourite genre. And whether writing about the distant or not so distant past, it was Wiltshire that was, endearingly, her lodestar: 'Wiltshire is, in my eyes, the most beautiful of English counties'.[1] Edith envisaged that Wiltshire history, broadly defined, would be the pinnacle of her literary life. In 1943, in response to an invitation to write a volume for a new County Books series, she confided to her journal that 'if I could do it well [it would be] something I would love to leave behind'. Adhering strictly her editor's remit to paint 'a true and lively picture of ... county and people', it was completed in October 1947 and published posthumously in 1951.[2]

It was her work in the wider community, however, for which Edith is most fondly remembered today. Two major foci of her attention during the inter-war years were the Council for the Preservation of Rural England and the Women's Institute. The former, established in 1926, could not fail but evoke Edith's sympathy. During the 1930s she served on the executive committee for Wiltshire; in 1932 she proposed that there should be a county anti-litter league.[3] Formed in 1915, Edith was even more active for the Women's Institute. She served on the committee of the Wiltshire Federation of Women's Institutes which was created in 1918, compiled booklets for members, and was much in demand as a branch speaker. Topics she worked up for presentations in 1929 included 'St Edith the Patron Saint of Wilton'. Amongst many others, Edith spoke to the Corsley branch on 'Danes in Wiltshire in Alfred's Day', in March 1925, and at Lacock, with 'native wit and humour', in June 1935. The latter audience were regaled on one of her favourite topics, 'Wiltshire dialects'.[4] Closer to home, and open to all genders, she took members of the Somerset Archaeological and Natural History Society around Wilton House, and even welcomed members of the Wiltshire

1   *Wiltshire Times*, 17 May 1938.
2   Middelboe, *Edith Olivier*, pp. 279, 308.
3   *Wiltshire Times*, 30 July 1932, 15 July 1939.
4   *Wiltshire Times*, 14 Mar. 1925, 2 Feb., 29 June 1935.

Archaeological Society to the Daye House.[1]

By far the greatest call on Edith's time was her work in local government. In 1934 she became the first woman ever to be elected to Wilton council. She threw herself into committee work – unglamorous work on housing and rates – whilst visits to the Mental Defectives Institute and Salisbury Workhouse removed any illusions she might have entertained about the lives of those less fortunate than herself.[2] Four years later, in November 1938, Edith was elected mayor, an elevation which attracted the attention even of the *Daily Mail*. Lord Pembroke wrote from Wilton House to congratulate 'my saintly Edith!' Her natural instincts for charity, history and performance were immediately apparent. Free coal was provided for pensioners that Christmas; she also revived the custom of Charity Bread, long since fallen into desuetude, by which 83 parishioners were given a loaf outside the old church on her birthday.[3]

Since Edith was re-elected each year until 1941, her mayoralty of Wilton coincided with one of the most challenging periods in the borough's history. But Edith was in her element. Cecil Beaton witnessed her in the North forecourt of Wilton House in March 1940. 'No half measures for Madame Mayor: she was clad in black and scarlet, complete with tricorn and buckled pumps, and contrived to combine, at the same time, the appearance of a Hogarthian lawyer and a blackbird'. Strutting like the proverbial peacock, she 'towers above the usual run of humanity'.[4] Her most pressing task when the Second World War broke out was coping with the influx of evacuees. As many as 141 turned up on a single night at Wilton in July 1940. Beaton recalled that Wilton House alone became home to 40 youngsters 'from the slums of Kentish town', their minds devoid of gaiety, and their hair full of nits. His verdict, that within just a few weeks, 'their cheeks became less pallid, their eyes brighter, and all of them were soon dry-nosed,

1   *Wiltshire Times*, 18 July 1925, 5 Aug. 1939.
2   Middelboe, *Edith Olivier*, p. 159.
3   Middelboe, *Edith Olivier*, pp. 206-8.
4   Beaton, *The Years Between. Diaries: 1939-44*, pp. 15-16.

clean-headed and smooth-skinned' was, perhaps, exaggerated. He had not had to face the administrative headache of placing the evacuees with hosts: residents could claim four times as much to host a soldier as they could to host a child. Edith found herself 'refereeing undignified contests over the sought-after military billetees, whilst at the same time trying not to let the mothers and children think that they were not welcome'.[1]

39. *Beatrice, Countess of Pembroke, and 15th Earl with General Claude Auchinleck and officers of Southern Command, 1940*

For all the daily strain she endured, Edith retained her sense of history. Hence her ambivalence when Wilton House was requisitioned as the Headquarters of Southern Command in June 1940. 'The war is actually being fought from that room', she reflected of the Double Cube. On the other hand, the necessity for the military to be ensconced there was 'a frightful barbarism worthy of Hitler'. The van Dycks and the myriad other treasures were now a 'legitimate objective for Hitler'.[2] But she

1 Middelboe, *Edith Olivier*, p. 232.
2 Middelboe, *Edith Olivier*, p. 233.

was unequivocal about what should be done as the possibility of invasion loomed that summer. Edith wrote to all Wilton households, exhorting them to invoke the spirt of King Alfred in 871 (the year he had resisted Danish invaders there), 'the spirit with which I think we should prepare to meet the trying days ahead'. Specifically, there should be no defeatism and no gossip. Women were instructed to employ their imagination and skill to ensure the best food for household members. 'Eat what you can and can what you can't', she suggested, would be a useful mantra. Above all, Wiltonians needed to remember the just cause in which they were engaged: 'Life up your hearts. Hold up your heads. Keep up your spirits and England will never go under'.[1]

Not every councillor appears to have appreciated Edith's theatrical style as mayor. She was not re-elected for another term in 1942, the year she turned 70. The years down to 1945, however, offered little respite. She was still a councillor and magistrate: on one traumatic occasion, acting in the latter capacity, she committed a soldier (he had just shot his sergeant) for murder. Her other roles during wartime included being director of the County Air Raid Precautions Executive, chair of the Wiltshire Cottage Improvement Society, president of the local St John Ambulance Brigade, and chair of the Wiltshire Citizens Advice Bureau.[2]

A month after V.E. Day, Edith spoke to the Civic Rights Association in Laverton. Her talk, in which she was able to draw upon her deep knowledge of Wiltshire's history and her own experience, reveals how she believed local government worked best, and why she had dedicated so much time to it: 'She continually stressed the fact that organisations should be kept small, in order that the members should have an intimate knowledge of the subject under discussion. Having had to attend small Committee meetings she had learnt many things from them. Too much centralisation was not good, because the people who discussed

1   *Wiltshire Times*, 27 July 1940.
2   *Wiltshire Times*, 6 Apr. 1940, 3 Feb. 1945.

the problems and control the policy would be out of touch with the actual problems on which they were basing their discussion'.[1] She regarded the Labour Party's landslide victory in the following month's general election as 'disastrous', a big leap on the wrong road to collectivism.

Edith would not live to see where that road would wend. Her health was failing; her appearances in public commensurately infrequent. Even so, she was able to deliver her talk on Wiltshire dialects to the women of the Wraxall Women's Institute in the spring of 1948. On April 28th, along with Sassoon and others, her name appeared as a signatory to a letter published in *The Times* objecting to the proposed construction of a new cement works just half a mile from the famous white horse at Westbury.[2] But following a series of strokes, Edith died, on May 10th 1948, aged 75.

A devout Christian and avid churchgoer – Edith had agreed to be secretary to the Bishop's Women's Diocesan Council as long ago as 1928 – she was buried four days later in an unpretentious grave in Wilton churchyard, close by her parents and her sister Mildred. A simple wooden cross marks the spot. In physical stature Edith was small, little more than five feet; to those who encountered her, however, she was in most other respects, a towering figure. The farmer, writer and broadcaster, A.G. Street, one of many to whom Edith offered advice on being an author, recalled that 'Edith Olivier was an irresistible force against which I dared not play the role of immovable object'.[3] Writing the same year, it was, perhaps, Cecil Beaton who best captured the essence of that 'irresistible force': 'it seems inconceivable ... that, from the vicarage in Wilton, this penniless spinster should create such ripples. Her energy and vitality are unlimited. She can talk or listen intently all day; she relates long stories with heroic gusto; she is witty and full of jokes. At night, she retires to read three books and write a detailed journal. Next morning, she appears as

1   *Wiltshire Times*, 16 June 1945.
2   *The Times*, 28 Apr. 1948; *Wiltshire Times*, 22 May 1948.
3   Middelboe, *Edith Olivier*, p. 123.

fresh as ever ... But it is, above all, Edith's understanding qualities that make her a boon to those who write or create in the other arts as well as to simple country folk. She has infinite sympathy. Everyone goes to her with troubles, knowing she can be trusted implicitly'.[1]

1   Beaton, *The Wandering Years. Diaries: 1922-1939*, p. 248-9.

Epilogue

Hope for the Future?

I N DEFERENCE TO those still living, we do not propose to comment in depth on those who have fashioned Wilton over the past half century or so. Nevertheless, readers may be interested in an outline of that story; some concluding reflections on where it had gone before, and a tentative suggestion about where it might lead in the future.

Mary Dorothea Hope, who married the 16th Earl of Pembroke in 1936, was born on December 31st 1903. Edith Olivier noted, with approval, that she and Mary shared the same birthday. Mary was the younger daughter of the Scottish nobleman, John Louis Hope, 7th Earl of Hopetoun, the first Governor-General of Australia, before being elevated in the peerage as 1st Marquess of Linlithgow in 1902. He died, aged 47, in 1908 when Mary was barely four years old. She was raised, therefore, principally by her mother, Hersey Alice Eveleigh de Moleyns, who indulged in the then decidedly unladylike pursuits of angling, hunting and shooting. As a young woman, Mary became a lady in waiting to Princess Marina, Duchess of Kent. This brought her into the orbit of Sidney, Lord Herbert, an equerry to the Duke.

The news that Mary was to marry Sidney was greeted warmly by friends and family. Edith Olivier, on first meeting her, found her 'So gay, so amusing, such a brilliant mimic'.[1] Their response was, sadly, part-based on the knowledge that Sidney had not got on well with his mother, the formidable Beatrice. She was said to have shown 'indifference' to him because, if

1   Middelboe, *Edith Olivier*, p. xvi.

39. *Lady Mary Hope c. 1936*

report is to be believed, he cried too much when he was three: 'she thought he was a bit of a failure thereafter'.[1] But few, if any, shared Beatrice's assessment. Lord Herbert was popular, refined and intelligent. Truth be told, it was more he, not his mother, who had taken the most aesthetic interest in the well-being of the family's art treasures when Wilton House was commandeered

1   Middelboe, *Edith Olivier*, pp. 182, 281.

by Southern Command in 1940. A suitable bride for a man who 'was extremely sensitive, and particularly affected by his mother's irrational feelings towards him', was deemed overdue reward.[1]

The wedding took place in Westminster Abbey on July 27th 1936. Mary wore 'a classical dress of ivory-tinted satin, with a high, round neckline, long tight-fitting sleeves, and a swathed belt of the material'. The Duke of Kent was best man.[2] Not long after the wedding, when the new Lady Herbert visited the Daye House for the first time, Edith Olivier was, if anything, more enchanted than she had been on first acquaintance. 'Her repose and dignity cover lots of observation. She *rollicks* with fun, can *roar* with laughter and imitated me walking with the Town Council.'[3] To Edith, Cecil Beaton and others, Mary could be deliciously indiscreet.

Mary became Countess when Sidney succeeded his father as 16th Earl in 1960. As was only too obvious, Wilton House was in need of a facelift following the ravages of war and the relative indifference of the 15th Earl and Countess in their dotage. The new Earl and his Countess duly rose to the challenge, notably with the cleaning of pictures and mending of furniture.[4] Cecil Beaton noted, approvingly, of a party that he attended at Wilton in September 1967 that 'The Pembrokes keep up the tradition of the Edwardian house-party'. He was amongst the twelve present who, having played croquet, retreated to the library to hear Princess Alice of Athlone regale them all with stories of her grandmother, Queen Victoria.[5] The Earl died eighteen months later; Mary survived him until January 16th 1995 when she died at the age of 91.

The 1960s, it might be argued, only really came to Wilton in 1969 when Henry, Lord Herbert, succeeded his father to become 17th Earl of Pembroke. Both Cecil Beaton and the

1   Middelboe, *Edith Olivier*, p. 182.
2   *The Times*, 28 July 1936
3   Middelboe, *Edith Olivier*, pp. 182-3.
4   Herbert, *Engaging Eccentrics*, p. 93.
5   C. Beaton, *Self-Portrait with Friends*, p. 389.

Dowager Beatrice had been discomfited when, three years earlier, he had married Claire Pelly. The future Countess was more than respectable, descended as she was from Sir John Pelly, a Governor of the Bank of England in the early Victorian period; she was, in addition, a great-granddaughter of Sir Henry Tate, the sugar merchant who established the eponymous Tate Gallery. Beatrice, however, expostulated, with scant regard for historical accuracy, that it was the first time a Herbert had married a commoner since the fourteenth century. Beaton described the bride as 'an upper class "beatnik" girl' and wondered how long it would be before the newlyweds removed the van Dycks to make way for lesser offerings by Andy Warhol.[1] He need not have worried. The 17th Earl oversaw a major, and much lauded, restoration of the house between 1987 and 1992. Acknowledging the realities of later twentieth century estate management, the 17th Earl was instrumental in establishing Wilton House Trust in 1983. The Trustees have since shouldered a good deal of the responsibility for maintenance issues. The Countess, meanwhile, assisted by Pat Burgess, a more recent occupant of the Daye House, made a distinctive mark on Wilton by establishing a Riding School for the Disabled. She also, after keeping Wilton on tenterhooks in producing three daughters, gave birth to a son, William, in 1978.[2]

William, Lord Herbert, duly became 18th Earl of Pembroke on the death of the 17th Earl in 2003.[3] There was to be no Countess at Wilton (the first break since 1874) until May 2010. The void was filled by Victoria Bullough. From Perthshire, she is the daughter of Michael and Sandra Bullough, owners of the Scottish department store, McEwens. Far more germane to Wilton's never-ending story, however, the Countess has a First Class degree in Interior Spatial Design. This has been utilised to

1   Vickers, *Cecil Beaton*, p. 505.
2   B. Allen, 'Two successful restorations. Wilton House and Frogmore House', *Apollo* (1990), pp. 336-9; Robinson, *Wilton House*, pp. 239-40.
3   The 17th Earl's first marriage was dissolved in 1981. He married Miranda Oram, an army officer's daughter and erstwhile kindergarten teacher, in 1988. The couple had three daughters.

the full as she and the Earl engage with the challenges of running a twenty first century stately home. The most significant project (2009-2012) of the recent past has been the reassembling of the 8th Earl's collection of antique statuary in Wyatt's Cloisters. For nearly 70 years after 1940, many pieces had languished outside, variously buried in undergrowth, reincarnated as garden containers and, in one case, subjected to the indignity of being deposited in the River Nadder.[1] More recently still, 'working closely with Lady P.', David Mlinaric, the renowned interior decorator, has undertaken a thoroughgoing programme of house repair and refurbishment. The fruits of their industry are most apparent in the revamped Georgian Dining Room, and the new crimson velvet curtains hanging under the Chippendale Rococo gilded pelmet boards in the State Rooms, as well as the rehanging of the 10th Earl's private apartment with moireed silk. None of the curtains had been replaced since Catherine Woronzow installed them in 1824.[2]

A newly-commissioned portrait of the Countess by Rupert Alexander shows her sitting beside a paper strewn table: 'The papers', she explains, 'represent all the projects, my drawings and illustrations for the work I have undertaken at Wilton.' The present Earl proudly acknowledges the contribution of his wife to the evolution of his family home. It will be for History to judge whether, as seems possible, the Countess will have been the most impactful on the interior décor of Wilton since her celebrated Russian predecessor.[3]

In giving birth to four children, it could be argued that the present Countess has made an even more significant contribution to the destiny of Wilton. More specifically, since two of them are boys, the current branch of the Herbert line is more secure than it has been for a century. The stark fact remains that the most significant task of Wilton's wives, if the Pembroke title is

1   Robinson, *Wilton House*, pp. 242-53.
2   Robinson, *Wilton House*, p. 253.
3   Unpublished notes to Wilton House guides from the Countess of Pembroke, 2 Apr. 2019; Robinson, *Wilton House*, p. 22.

to survive, is to produce sons. In this, they have been remarkably successful. This is no mere platitude. Britain's aristocracy is not as immutable as one might suppose; the vast majority of titles date only from the Victorian period. Dating from 1551, the Pembroke earldom is the fourth oldest in the country.[1] Further, the Herberts (since 1630 when Philip, Earl of Montgomery succeeded as 4th Earl of Pembroke) are one of only four families who can boast two earldoms in the same person.

A further criterion by which one could measure the relative significance of the women in the present study is by the wealth which they brought to the estate. The major contributors in this respect were Margaret Sawyer and Mary Fitzwilliam. Both windfalls were the more welcome since they were available when the 7th and 10th Earl's conduct had rendered Wilton's finances precarious.[2] And without Anne Parr's marriage to the 1st Earl, of course, there might never have been a Herbert Wilton estate at all, and certainly not one as large. And some Countesses, for instance Beatrice Paget, deserve applause because they did more than their spouses to keep that estate together. Others, like Catherine Woronzow, complemented the work of their husbands, in working to rebuild and maintain it. One or two, Elizabeth Spencer and Catherine Woronzow, even if clandestinely, reputedly saved treasures for the Wilton collection from Earls (10th and 12th), whose profligacy would probably have led to their being sold. Paradoxically, therefore, the Herbert wives have sometimes been more loyal and devoted to Wilton than their Herbert husbands.

Assuredly not all Herbert wives were paragons, though it is hard to fix on one who especially failed in her duties. The same cannot be said for their husbands. Even when allowance is made for a society whose mores tolerated a degree of male infidelity, the 10th Earl's behaviour, in hurting the seemingly unimpeachable Betty Spencer, earned him widespread notoriety. And though the

---

1   There are currently 191 earldoms in the United Kingdom.
2   Neglecting the estate, of which the incumbent Earl was viewed as the trustee for future generations, was the most heinous of crimes, far more so than marital infidelity.

homicidal 7th Earl is not recorded as having done any physical harm to Henriette de Kérouaille, he was clearly somebody best avoided. But surely none was treated so badly by the Herbert family as Octavia Spinelli? The wives have certainly been more sinned against than sinning.

Conversely, it should be recognised that even in earlier ages, when dynastic considerations predominated, a number of women who came to Wilton found themselves entering happy marriages. High on the list of worthy husbands we might number the 8th, 9th, 11th and 16th Earls.[1] But an indulgent husband, even perhaps an indifferent one, could allow his spouse to make her mark on the world: one need only think of the 2nd Earl and Mary Sidney. To pursue the point in a slightly different direction, it is not perhaps entirely coincidental that Florence Nightingale and Edith Olivier never married.

It would be patently ridiculous to claim that all the women considered here were exceptional. Birth, wealth and title conferred on them an automatic prominence in society. Before the twentieth century, at least, the concomitant privilege which they enjoyed incurred responsibilities which they were more or less obliged to discharge as an accepted part of their role in a hierarchical society. Put another way, Wilton's women, as explored here, were bound to be significant figures in the household, the town, and on the wider estate, quite probably within Wiltshire too. Whether they became significant beyond the county borders was far more a question of character and ability. That is why Mary Sidney and (of our 'honourary' Wilton women), Florence Nightingale stand head and shoulders above the others in our study. Collectively, however, at the risk of being tendentious, Wilton's women might be said to have made more of a mark than its men. In a judgement which was surprisingly frank for the deferential 1860s, John Sanford and Meredith Townsend concluded that the Herberts 'have, on the whole, done less for England than most of her

---

1   And, of course, the 18th Earl!

40. Wilton House from the south side of the River Nadder showing the seventeenth century south front and Palladian Bridge (author's collection)

older houses'.[1] They might fairly have added that it is difficult to think of a family which has provided a home for so many notable women.

So far as the future is concerned, the most common question asked by today's visitor is what will happen at Wilton should the law be altered to allow the first born child (as opposed to the first born son) to succeed to the Pembroke title? Our answer, on the basis of the present survey, is that all will be well.

1   J.L. Sanford & M. Townsend, *The Great Governing Families of England*, II, p. 189. The point that the authors were making was that Sidney Herbert, who had only died in 1861, had scaled the political heights without the benefit of the Pembroke title. It is a moot point that the Herberts more generally had been any more or less worthy than their aristocratic counterparts.

Appendix. Wilton Wives

Name	Countess of Pembroke	Spouse	Married	Children
Anne Parr (1515-1552)	1551-1552	William, 1st Earl (1506-1570)	c. 1538	2s , 1 da., mother of 2nd Earl
Ann Talbot (15??-1588)	1552-1570	William, 1st Earl (1506-1570)	1552	d.s.p.
Catherine Grey (1540-1568)	n/a	Henry, 2nd Earl (1539-1601)	1553	d.s.p.
Katherine Talbot (c.1552-1576)	1562-1576	Henry, 2nd Earl (1539-1601)	1562	d.s.p.
Mary Sidney (1561-1621)	1577-1601	Henry, 2nd Earl (1539-1601)	1577	2s, 2da. (1 d.v.p.) mother of 3rd & 4th Earl
Mary Talbot (c.1580-1650)	1604-1630	William, 3rd Earl (1580-1630)	1604	1s d.v.p.
Susan de Vere (1587-1629)	n/a	Philip, 4th Earl (1584-1649)	1604	6s (1 d.v.p.), 3 da. (2 d.v.p.), mother of 5th Earl
Anne Clifford (1590-1676)	1630-1649	Philip, 4th Earl (1584-1649)	1630	d.s.p.

Name	Countess of Pembroke	Spouse	Married	Children
Penelope Naunton (1620-1647)	n/a	Philip, 5th Earl (1621-1669)	1639	1s, mother of 6th Earl
Catherine Villiers (c. 1634-c. 1678)	1649-1669	Philip, 5th Earl (1621-1669)	1649	2s, 4da. (1 *d.v.p.*), mother of 7th and 8th Earl
n/a	n/a	William, 6th Earl (1640-1674)	un-married	n/a
Henriette de Kérouaille (1650-1728)	1675-1683	Philip, 7th Earl (1653-1683)	1675	1 da.
Margaret Sawyer (1657-1706)	1684-1706	Thomas, 8th Earl (1656-1733)	1684	7s, 5da., mother of 9th Earl
Barbara Slingsby (1668-1721)	1708-1721	Thomas, 8th Earl (1656-1733)	1708	2da.
Mary Howe (c. 1703-1749)	1725-1733	Thomas, 8th Earl (1656-1733)	1725	*d.s.p.*
Mary Fitzwilliam (1707-1769)	1733-1750	Henry, 9th Earl (1692-1750)	1733	1s, mother of 10th Earl
Elizabeth Spencer (1737-1831)	1756-1794	Henry, 10th Earl (1734-1794)	1756	1s, 1da. (*d.v.p.*), mother of 11th Earl
Elizabeth Beauclerk (1769-1793)	n/a	George, 11th Earl (1759-1827)	1787	3s (2 *d.v.p.*), 1da., mother of 12th Earl

Name	Countess of Pembroke	Spouse	Married	Children
Catherine Woronzow (1783-1856)	1808-1827	George, 11th Earl (1759-1827)	1808	1s (Sidney), 5da., grandmother of 13th & 14th Earl
Octavia Spinelli (1779-1857)	1814-1857	Robert, 12th Earl (1791-1862)	1814	*d.s.p.*
Elizabeth à Court (1822-1911)	n/a	Sidney Herbert, Lord Herbert of Lea (1810-1861)	1846	4s (1 *d.v.p.*), 3 da., mother of 13th and 14th Earl
Gertrude Talbot (1840-1906)	1874-1895	George, 13th Earl (1850-1895)	1874	*d.s.p.*
Beatrix Lambton (1859-1944)	1895-1913	Sidney, 14th Earl (1853-1913)	1877	2s, 2da., mother of 15th Earl
Beatrice Paget (1883-1973)	1913-1960	Reginald, 15th Earl (1880-1960)	1904	3s, 2da. mother of 16th Earl
Mary Hope (1903-1995)	1960-1969	Sidney, 16th Earl (1906-1969)	1936	1s, 1da., mother of 17th Earl.
Claire Pelly (b. 1943)	1969-1981	Henry, 17th Earl (1939-2003)	1966	1s, 3da., mother of 18th Earl
Miranda Oram (b. 1962)	1988-2003	Henry, 17th Earl (1939-2003)	1988	3 da.
Victoria Bullough (b. 1985)	2010-	William, 18th Earl (b. 1978)	2010	2s, 2 da.

Select Bibliography

Bodleian Library, Oxford
Manning Papers
British Library
Gladstone Papers
Herbert of Lea Papers
Nightingale Papers
Stanmore Papers
Hartley Library, Southampton University
Broadlands Papers
Lambeth Palace
Talbot Papers
National Archives
Court of Chancery Records
West Sussex Record Office, Chichester
Goodwood Papers
Wiltshire and Swindon History Centre, Chippenham
Pembroke Papers
Olivier Papers

Newspapers and Periodicals
Apollo
Country Life
Devizes and Wiltshire Gazette
Hampshire Chronicle
Illustrated London News
Salisbury Journal
Tatler
The Times
Western Times

Books and Articles. Place of publication is London unless stated
Adamson, Donald & Beauclerk Dewar, Peter, *The House of Nell Gwyn.*
   The Fortunes of the Beauclerk Family, 1670-1974, 1974
Allen, Julia, & Bennett, Christine, *Mary Sidney Herbert Countess of*

Pembroke. An Elizabethan Writer and her World, Gloucester, 2022

Beaton, Cecil, *Cecil Beaton Diaries*, 4 vols, 1961-1973

Beckett, J.V., *The Aristocracy in England, 1660-1914*, Oxford, 1988

Bernard, G.W., *The Power of the Early Tudor Nobility. A Study of the Fourth and Fifth Earls of Shrewsbury*, Brighton, 1985

Bevan, Frances, *The Ladies of Lydiard*, Gloucester, 2021

Bostridge, Mark, *Florence Nightingale The Woman and Her Legend*, 2008

Brennan, Michael G., *Literary Patronage in the English Renaissance: The Pembroke Family*, 1988.

Buckle, Richard (ed.), *Self-Portrait with Friends. The Selected Dairies of Cecil Beaton 1926-1974*, 1982

Cannadine, David, *The Decline and Fall of the British Aristocracy*, 1990

Clark, Andrew (ed.) *'Brief Lives', chiefly of Contemporaries, set down by John Aubrey, between the years 1669 & 1696*, Oxford, 2 vols, 1898

Clifford, D.J.H. (ed.), *The Diaries of Lady Anne Clifford*, Stroud, 1990

Cook, Sir Edward, *The Life of Florence Nightingale*, 2 vols, 1913.

Cutting, B.M., 'A countess transformed: how Lady Susan Vere became Lady Anne Clifford,' *Brief Chronicles*, IV (2012–13), pp. 117–34

de Lisle, Leanda, *The Sisters Who Would be Queen: The Tragedy of Mary, Katherine & Lady Jane Grey*, 2009.

Dossey, B.M., *Florence Nightingale: Mystic, Visionary, Healer*, Philadelphia, 2010

Foreman, Amanda, *Georgiana, Duchess of Devonshire*, 1998

Forneron, H., *Louise de Kerouaille, Duchess of Portsmouth*, 4th ed., 1891.

Forster, Margaret, *Significant Sisters. The Grassroots of Active Feminism 1839-1939*, 1986

Foster, R.E., *Sidney Herbert. Too Short a Life*, Gloucester, 2019

Foster, R.E., 'Remembering Sidney Herbert: A Statuesque History', *Sarum Chronicle*, XX (2020), pp. 7-22

Fraser, Antonia, *The Case of the Married Woman. Caroline Norton: A 19th-Century Woman who wanted justice for women*, 2021

Freer, Coburn, 'The Countess of Pembroke in a World of Words', *Style*, V (1971), pp. 37-56

Goldie, S.M. (ed.), *"I have done my duty." Florence Nightingale in the Crimean War 1854-1856*, Manchester, 1987

Guilding, Ruth, 'Grecian Gods and Demi-Gods in Niches … Fit for the Castle of Otranto', *Apollo*, 154 (2001), pp. 42-48

Herbert, David, *Second Son. An Autobiography*, 1972

Herbert, David, *Engaging Eccentrics. Recollections*, 1990

Herbert, Lord (ed.), The *Pembroke Papers (1734-1780). Letters and Diaries of Henry, Tenth Earl of Pembroke and his Circle*, 1939

Herbert, Lord (ed.), *Pembroke Papers (1780-1794). Letters and Diaries of Henry, Tenth Earl of Pembroke and his Circle*, 1950

Herbert, Lady Elizabeth, *How I Came Home*, 1894

Herbert, Lady Elizabeth, *Anglican Prejudices Against the Catholic Church*, 1899

Hicks, Carola, *Improper Pursuits. The Scandalous Life of Lady Di Beauclerk*, 2001

Hollis, Stephanie (ed.), *Writing the Wilton Women. Goscelin's Legend of Edith and the Liber confortatorius*, Turnhout, Belgium, 2004

Holmes, Martin, *Proud Northern Lady*, Chichester, 1975

James, Susan, *Catherine Parr: Henry VIII's Last Love*, Stroud, 2009.

Lawrence, Raleigh St, 'Lady Elizabeth Herbert of Lea', *Sarum Chronicle*, I, 2000, pp. 37-43

Lamb, Mary Ellen, 'The Countess of Pembroke's Patronage', *English Literary Renaissance*, XII (1982), pp. 162-79.

Lees-Milne, James, *Earls of Creation. Five Great Patrons of Eighteenth-Century Art*, 1962

Lever, Tresham, *The Herberts of Wilton*, 1967

Lewis, W.S. (ed.), *The Yale Edition of Horace Walpole's Correspondence*, 48 vols, New Haven, 1937-1983

Lovell, Mary S., *Bess of Hardwick, First Lady of Chatsworth*, 2006

Luck, Kate, 'The growing pains of the "Women on the Land movement" in Wiltshire 1914-1917: recruitment and training women before the formation of the Women's Land Army', *The Local Historian*, XLVII (2017), pp. 193-207

Martienssen, A. *Queen Catherine Parr*, 1975

Middelboe, Penelope (ed.), *Edith Olivier. From her Journals 1924-48*, 1989

Mingay, G.E., *English Landed Society in the Eighteenth Century*, 1963

Nicolson, Adam, *Earls of Paradise. England: the dream of Perfection*, 2008

Olivier, Edith, *Without Knowing Mr Walkley: Personal Memories*, 1938

Olivier, Edith, *Wiltshire*, 1951

Osherow, Michele, 'Mary Sidney's embroidered psalms', *Renaissance Studies*, XXIX (2015), pp. 650-70

Oxford Dictionary of National Biography, Oxford, 2004

Pembroke, 13th Earl of, *The Earl and the Doctor, South Sea Bubbles*, New York, 1872

Porter, Linda, *Katherine the Queen*, 2012

Pugh, R.B., and Crittall, Elizabeth (eds.), *The Victoria History of Wiltshire*, vol. 3, 1956

Roberts, Josephine A., 'Mary Sidney, Countess of Pembroke', *English*

Literary Renaissance, XIV (1984), pp. 426-39

Robinson, John Martin, 'Regency Revival: the 19th-Century Refurnishing of Wilton', *Apollo*, CLXX (2009), pp. 42-47

Robinson, John Martin, *Requisitioned: The British Country House in the Second World War*, 2014

Robinson, John Martin, *Wilton House. The Art, Architecture and Interiors of One of Britain's Great Stately Homes*, New York, 2021

Russell, Francis, *A Catalogue of the Pictures and Drawings at Wilton House*, Oxford, 2021

Sanford, John Langton, & Townsend, Meredith, *The Great Governing Families of England*, 2 vols, 1865

Scarisbrick, J.J., *Henry VIII*, 1968

Sharpe, Kevin, *Criticism and Compliment. The Politics of Literature in the England of Charles I*, Cambridge, 1987

Spence, R.T., *Lady Anne Clifford: countess of Pembroke, Dorset and Montgomery, 1590–1676*, 1997

Stanmore, Lord, *Sidney Herbert. Lord Herbert of Lea. A Memoir*, 2 vols, 1906

Starkey, David, *Six Wives. The Queens of Henry VIII*, 2003

Stewart, Peter, *A Catalogue of the Sculpture Collection at Wilton House*, Oxford, 2020

Thomas, Sheila R., 'Captain Augustus Montgomery, RN (1762-1797): Wiltshire's forgotten aristocratic bastard', *Wiltshire Archaeological and Natural History Magazine*, CI (2008), pp. 213-25

Thomas, Sheila R., 'Care in the Community: an example from 19th-century Wiltshire', *Wiltshire Archaeological and Natural History Magazine*, CII (2009), pp. 296-305

Thomasson, Anna, *A Curious Friendship. The Story of a Bluestocking and a Bright Young Thing*, 2015

Thompson, F.M.L., *English Landed Society in the Nineteenth Century*, 1963

Vickers, Hugo, *Cecil Beaton. The Authorised Biography*, 1985

Vickers, Hugo, *The Unexpurgated Beaton. The Cecil Beaton Diaries as he wrote them, 1970-1980*, 2002

Vickery, Amanda, *The Gentleman's Daughter. Women's Lives in Georgian England*, 1998

Williams, Penry, *The Later Tudors. England, 1547-1603*, Oxford, 1995

Woolley, Sonia, 'Without knowing Miss Olivier', *Sarum Chronicle*, XVI (2016), pp.116-23

Young, Frances, *Mary Sidney, Countess of Pembroke*, 1912

Index